THE FIVE SOLAS OF THE REFORMATION

BY ANDY MCILREE

Published by:

Hayes Press

The Barn, Flaxlands

Royal Wootton Bassett

Swindon, SN4 8DY

United Kingdom

www.hayespress.org

Copyright © Hayes Press 2019

Table of Contents

The Five Solas of the Reformation 1

Chapter One: Introduction 2

Chapter Two: Sōlā Scrīptūrā – Scripture Alone 6

Chapter Three: Solus Christus – Christ Alone 18

Chapter Four: Sōlā Grātiā - Grace Alone 28

Chapter Five: Sōlā Fidē - By Faith Alone 39

Chapter Six: Solī Deō Gloria – The Glory of God Alone 51

Appendix 1: The Ninety-five Theses by Luther 62

Appendix 2: Luther's Speech at the Imperial Diet in Worms, Germany (April 1521) 71

Chapter One: Introduction

When Martin Luther's hammer drummed on the door of the Castle Church in Wittenberg on 31st October 1517, the sound of nailing his Ninety-five Theses (see Appendix 1) to it thundered through the Vatican and echoed all the way to the ears of Pope Leo X. At that moment, the accompanying lightning strike lit up the dark religious sky, and heralded the dawn of Christian recovery that has continued for over five hundred years. It's a day that should be etched on every Christian's heart and mind with a real sense of indebtedness. Luther's theses, which roundly condemned beliefs and practices of the Roman Catholic Church, were timely for it was in the same year, 1517, that Pope Leo offered indulgences to everyone who donated money for the rebuilding of Saint Peter's Basilica in Rome.

There's no doubt that this triggered Luther's response and gave him further justification to include No.28 of his theses which says, "It is certain that when money clinks in the money chest, greed and avarice can be increased; but when the church intercedes, the result is in the hands of God alone." It seems that his choice of words was an intentional echo of an exaggerated announcement made by Johann Tetzel, a Dominican Friar, who promised, "As soon as a coin in the coffer rings, a soul from Purgatory springs."

Sadly, this kind of thinking wasn't left behind five centuries ago, for it actually reared its head, and for a very different reason, toward the middle of 2018. Pope Francis gave a similar promise of "plenary indulgences", meaning a reduced time in Purgatory as punishment for sins. The announcement from the Vatican was clear: "Catholics who participate in the World Meeting of Families in Dublin or pray with their families during the August 21 to 26 event can receive a plenary indulgence." The statement went on to say, "So that the faithful prepare spiritually to participate in the event in the best way, His Holiness Pope Francis willingly concedes the gift of indulgences." The decree was released on May 22 by the Vatican Dicastery (1) for Laity, the Family and Life and reported in the Catholic Herald on 24th May 2018.

Three and a half years of turmoil followed Luther's action of impaling his Ninety-Five Theses to the church door, and on 17th April 1521 he was summoned to face the charge of heresy at the Diet of Worms in Germany. His speech was eloquent, bold and uncompromising (see Appendix 2). On his way back to Wittenberg, he was 'kidnapped' by the arrangement of his defender, Frederick the Wise, and taken to Wartburg Castle where he began his work of translating the New Testament from Greek into the German language, and completing it in eleven weeks. Taking full advantage of the printing press, he had it ready for distribution ten months later in 1522, and the whole Bible was available in 1534. This was yet another challenge to the claims of the Roman Catholic Church that the Bible is not self-sufficient and does not determine its own contents, vouch for its own inspiration, or interpret itself.

Pope Leo X restated this by saying, "No person shall preach without the permission of his Superior. All preachers shall explain the Gospel according to the Fathers." They believed the Bible is God's gift to the Church, which is its custodian and authoritative interpreter. By contrast, Luther and the Reformers were of the view that God's Word should be in the hands of the people, that Scripture is its own interpreter, and that the Spirit of God would be their Teacher. It was in the belief that they should be reliant on Him that the Reformation held firmly to the first cry of the Five Solas – Sōlā Scrīptūrā.

Five centuries later, is there still a need for reformation? Yes, definitely. Luther's Ninety-Five Theses could still be nailed to the doors of the Vatican, the Reformers' Five Solas should be engraved on all our hearts, and the need could hardly be greater for them to be nailed to the doors of many churches. There is so much shallowness in Christian churches, and they are in danger of going *"into captivity"* and *"are destroyed for lack of knowledge"* (Isa.5:13; Hos.4:6).

(1) A dicastery (from Greek δικαστήριον, law-court, from δικαστής, judge/juror) is a department of the Roman Curia, the administration of the Holy See through which the pope directs the Roman Catholic Church.

A mighty fortress is our God,
A bulwark never failing:
Our helper He, amid the flood
Of mortal ills prevailing.
For still our ancient foe
Doth seek to work his woe;
His craft and power are great,
And armed with cruel hate,
On earth is not his equal.

Did we in our own strength confide,
Our striving would be losing;
Were not the right Man on our side,
The Man of God's own choosing.
You ask who that may be?
Christ Jesus, it is He;
Lord Sabaoth is His name,
From age to age the same,
And He must win the battle.

And though this world, with devils filled,
Should threaten to undo us,
We will not fear, for God hath willed
His truth to triumph through us.
The Prince of Darkness grim,
We tremble not for him;
His rage we can endure,
For lo! His doom is sure,—
One little word shall fell him.

That word above all earthly powers,
No thanks to them, abideth;
The Spirit and the gifts are ours
Through Him who with us sideth.
Let goods and kindred go,
This mortal life also:
The body they may kill:
God's truth abideth still,
His kingdom is forever.
(Martin Luther)

Chapter Two: Sōlā Scrīptūrā – Scripture Alone

In days of spiritual darkness and weakness, the five Solas of the Reformation were intended to be seen as shafts of light and pillars of biblical strength, with their stability and glory reflecting great truths from the Epistle to the Romans. It was vital to the Reformers that the inspired Word and their clarion calls would go inseparably together, and we begin our journey through the different aspects of truth they so preciously recovered with their five objectives in mind. To help us do this, we do well to look first at Hebrews chapter nine, verses nine and ten.

The writer had been discussing the glories of the Lord Jesus entering the Holy Place and contrasting it with the Old Testament service with its sacrifices and offerings that pointed forward to Him. Then he emphasised its importance by saying:

> *"It was symbolic for the present time in which both gifts and sacrifices are offered which cannot make him who performed the service perfect in regard to the conscience – concerned only with foods and drinks, various washings, and fleshly ordinances imposed until the time of reformation."*

If we go back to chapter four verse 12, we read God's high estimation of Scripture:

> *"For the word of God is living and powerful, and sharper than any two-edged sword, piercing even to the division of soul and spirit, and of joints and marrow, and is a discerner of the thoughts and intents of the heart."*

By combining these two portions, we are left in no doubt that it is the infallibility of divine revelation that forms and reforms how He should be served. As a keen searcher of God's Word, Martin Luther knew that his objectors had no regard for New Covenant freedom and no appreciation of how God delivers those who trust in "a different gospel" (1) by reforming them through "the gospel of Christ" (2).

If we take the five Solas that are identified with the Reformation, which began 500 years ago, we will see that Martin Luther was convicted and convinced that the service he had been performing as a monk was completely at odds with the Word of God. And so he drafted his ninety-five theses and made his way to the Castle Church in Wittenberg, which now takes his name as Lutherstadt Wittenberg, and nailed them to the door to let the Roman Catholic Church know how far removed it was from the truth of God's Word.

As the Reformation progressed, the five Solas were defined as:

1. Sōlā scrīptūrā - Scripture Alone

2. Solus Christus - Christ Alone

3. Sōlā grātiā - Grace Alone

4. Sōlā fidē - By Faith Alone

5. Solī Deō Gloria - The Glory of God Alone

Truths associated with these five standard-bearers of divine revelation gripped the heart of Luther and others, such as Philip Melancthon, Huldrych Zwingli and John Calvin, and yet, even before them, John Wycliffe and Jan Hus had become opposed to the Roman Catholic system and were longing for the Scriptures to be translated from Latin into local languages, so that they would be taken away from the clergy of the church and made available to the common people.

It's as if they were thinking of David's five stones, and of how one was enough to slay the giant. These five wonderful statements come to us from hard-fought times, including the Thirty Years' War of 1618-1648 during which, according to reports, eight million people lost their lives. A century earlier, Johannes Gutenberg invented the printing press and, hand-in-hand with the conviction of spiritual things that were necessary, they recognised that what God had formed in the early days of The Acts of the Apostles had become deformed and needed to be reformed.

When we read through our Bibles, we read about forming when God formed man of the dust of the earth (3), and about the *"people I have formed for Myself; They shall declare my praise"* (4). God also speaks about conforming and transforming (5). Only one verse speaks of reforming, yet it soon became evident that some assemblies knew of many who specialised in deforming. Paul described them as being in the corrupt business of *"peddling the word"* (6), by which he meant they were conmen who tricked people into believing and accepting the wrong interpretation of what scripture actually means. In contrast, he commended those in the assembly for being *"sincere"* (Gr. *eilikrinēs*), as if to say that their motives were so pure they were 'judged by sunlight'. What a high commendation!

Another defect is found in those whom Peter labelled as twisters (Gr. *strebloō*): people who bent every part of God's Word out of shape to suit their perverted thinking. The New Testament closes with the Lord's own review of seven churches, among whom only two, Smyrna and Philadelphia, were not guilty of some sort of spiritual deformity. If only the Faithful and True Witness could have told all seven, *"you are rich"* (7) and assured them, *"you ... have kept My word, and have not denied My name"* (8). So these early churches themselves proved to be the seedbed of deformed belief and practice.

Of course, this kind of wilful deforming accelerated in successive centuries and by the time of Luther there had been a landslide away from the truth of God through corrupting His Word. How well the Reformers knew that a real working of the Holy Spirit was needed if they were to see the inspired Word exalted to its proper place, and they firmly believed that only the reality of plenary inspiration could conquer the deformity of plenary indulgences. Three centuries later, Charles Spurgeon expressed the same kind of conviction when he said, "Defend the Bible? I'd sooner defend a lion! Let it loose, let it loose."

The Word became flesh

When the Lord Jesus Christ came into this world, unlike all the prophets who spoke the word, He was the Word (9) and, unlike them, He was more than a godly man for He was God manifested in the flesh (10). We should note how quickly, and simply, John established the uniqueness of the Word in the first four verses of his Gospel by contrasting the One who was not created with things that were. He did this by using two different Greek words for "was".

Four times, in verses 1 and 2, he consistently chose the word *ēn*, which is from the word *eimi* and forms part of his many references to Jesus as the I AM – *egō eimi*. His evident intention was to present Him as the eternal One who was, and is, and always will be, and he confirms this by using the word *egeneto* in verse 3 when referring to what "was made". Having done this, he then twice reverted to the word *ēn* in verse 4 to stress that the eternal One who is both life and light was not made. How wonderful it is that we are possessed, and possess, the Incarnate Word for He is the Man who is central to the message of the inspired Word!

The inspired Word

Paul referred to this when he wrote to young Timothy saying that "*All Scripture is given by inspiration of God*" (11) and here's the thought - not only that God would breathe into the words that men wrote, but that He actually breathed out the words that were written. It is a totally different concept that God breathed out these words and men wrote them, rather than the Word of God came of men or from men. Peter sums it up perfectly by assuring us that "*men of God spoke as they were moved* [carried along] *by the Holy Spirit*" (12).

In the days of the Reformation there were men who sensed the working of the Holy Spirit in their lives and they wanted to get back to the realities of the Word. This meant acknowledging three things:

- It is the word of God – He is its only source
- It is the word of the Lord – He is its only authority
- It is the word of Christ – He is its whole character

Besides these, God expresses it in many other ways. He refers to it as:

- the word of the gospel - Acts 15:7
- the word of His grace - Acts 20:32
- the word of the Cross - 1 Cor.1:18
- the word of reconciliation - 2 Cor.5:19
- the word of life – Phil.2:16
- the word of righteousness – Heb.5:13
- the word of truth – Jas.1:18

By taking all these aspects together, we see how they unite to express the initial three presentations, that the Scriptures are the Word of God, the Word of the Lord, and the Word of Christ. Through them, therefore, we bow in worship before their Source, and also are subject to their authority and character. By doing this, we show that we have confidence in the plenary inspiration, inerrancy, and complete infallibility of Scripture. From Genesis to Revelation God is revealing all the facets of His own Being, and that's the wonder of it. We have inerrancy, because we have an inerrant God, an inerrant Lord and an inerrant Christ. The infallibility of the Word of God rests on the infallibility of the God of the Word. The authority of the Word of the Lord rests on the authority of the Lord of the Word, and the character of the Word of Christ rests on the character of the Christ of God. Without Them, none of the other features of the Word of God could ever be enjoyed. The question is, how much time do we spend enjoying it?

The primacy of the Word

In Luther's day, they saw the need to recover the place for the Word of God and isn't it marvellous that you and I can pick up our Bibles at any time and study them for as long as we choose? The danger is that our familiarity with the Word means that we don't study it enough privately or give it sufficient place publicly in our churches. In spite of having been embedded in the Roman Catholic system, these men were the opposite. They were deeply moved by the Spirit of God and thought the Scriptures needed to be brought back to the forefront as they were in the New Testament church age. They were concerned about what should be vital in church life:

- to give the Word of God its proper place
- to see the primacy of the Word of God
- to discover or rediscover its power
- to know more about the preaching of the Word
- to see more about the Person in the Word
- and to be helped by other persons with the Word.

There's a lovely picture in 2 Chronicles 17:7-9, when Jehoshaphat became king and initiated days of recovery that were like a time of reformation, by appointing five leaders who were accompanied by ten Levites and 2 priests. All seventeen made their way through the cities of Judah and took the Law of the Lord with them. No, it wasn't a nice tiny edition that could be put into a pocket somewhere; they were carrying a scroll. Had anyone asked where they were going, they would have been told, "We are going down this street to talk to people about the Law of God." That was their ministry. As Levitical and leading men, they fulfilled their priestly responsibility of taking the Word of God out among the people of God. Luther, and others, had something similar in mind, and the challenge comes right down to us in our day – are we?

The delights of showing our love for the Word will be seen in our worship, and how essential this is! There's something far wrong, if our enjoyment of the Word isn't first expressed upwardly to God as "the fruit of lips which make confession to His name" (13), but the genuineness of our worship ought to flow into our witness inwardly to the people of God and then outwardly to others. In this way, we give the Word its place, show its primacy, experience its power, participate in it preaching and practice, we present the wonderful Person of our Lord Jesus Christ, and we fulfil our ministry as men and women of the Book!

The power of the Word

The Lord Jesus spoke rather firmly to Sadducees who believed there is no resurrection and, knowing their opinion, He told them, *"You are mistaken, not knowing the Scriptures nor the power of God"* (14). How well He knew that these two things go together. You see what he did? He combined the Word of God and the power of God. And He still says, that if we want to know the power of God we need the Word of God. Otherwise, we also make the same fundamental error.

When He rose from the dead and made that journey with the couple on the way to their home in Emmaus, what did He talk about? He didn't give them a graphic re-run of His sufferings, like some modern movie, but *"beginning at Moses and all the Prophets, He expounded to them in all the Scriptures the things concerning Himself"* (15). He is the man who has given us the title of *Sōlā Scrīptūrā* – the Incarnate Word with the inspired Word! In resurrection, this was His focus, His primacy to speak to them about seeing the Person in the Word, and He used the Old Testament to do it. The New Testament hadn't even begun, and He gave the best example of how we should get back to the written Word and be immersed in it. What was the result? Without any prompting, they openly confessed, *"Did not our heart burn within us while He talked with us on the road, and while He opened the Scriptures to us?" (16).*

Think of them heading back to Jerusalem; having already decided it was too late for Him to go on, they decided it wasn't too late for them to go back. It was not only that He had spoken *"to them"* (v.27); He shared the Word *"with"* them (v.32). That was the secret! They heard the Word of God and felt the power of God for He not only *"opened the Scriptures,"* (v.32) *"their eyes were opened"* too (v.31). Later, when He appeared to His disciples, *"He opened their understanding, that they might comprehend the Scriptures"* (v.45). They were so moved by what they had heard on the journey and in their home that they made their way back to Jerusalem, undoubtedly recounting as they went the things He divulged on the way. There are real lessons here for us. If hearts are to burn, and eyes and understanding opened, we must seek the Holy Spirit's help, so that we not only speak "to" people, but follow the Lord's example of speaking "with" them.

What better, then, could the early church do than follow His example? The Lord's earthly ministry had just come to an end, theirs had only begun, and it's evident that their sense of mission was based on His. Recognising that emulating His imparting of the Word was a vital part of the spiritual foundation, the apostles set out to ensure that they would fulfil their ministry toward those who were saved, baptised and added to the church in Jerusalem. When the challenge arose in Acts 6 of satisfying the practical needs of both Hebrews and Hellenists, the apostles were so concerned that they called for the church to select *"seven men of good reputation, full of the Holy Spirit and wisdom, whom we may appoint over this business"* (v.3).

Their reason is both enlightening and relevant to the present testimony of the churches: *"It is not desirable that we should leave the word of God and serve tables"* (v.2). It's enlightening, because it elevated the vital over the important; and relevant, because there's nothing in church life and responsibility that should cause leaders to *"leave the word of God"*. Yes, meeting social need is important, but not so important that it preoccupies those whose God-given charge is spiritually to *"feed the church of God"* (17).

This is why Paul took up similar language and urged us to *"give attention to reading, to exhortation, to doctrine ... for in doing this you will save both yourself and those who hear you"* (18). So, reading and exhortation and doctrine are irreplaceable, if we want to save ourselves. Lack of desire for the Word indicates that we have lost our desire to save our personal testimony and walk. God has called us to devote ourselves to exemplary lives of faithfulness and holiness (19) but the degree to which we are in the Word will determine the degree to which we save ourselves, and to which we allow the Spirit of God to assist us in the matter of seeing others saved too. Paul wasn't speaking only about the salvation of souls. He was speaking about the salvation of saints' lives through obedience and perseverance, and warning against the possibility of not having an adequate amount of reading, exhortation and reliance on expository teaching of the Word, so that we fail to save ourselves as individuals and assemblies ought to be doing. Fulfilling this will help us to be examples of what new believers should strive to be in their lives too.

When Paul was fulfilling his ministry, he *"vigorously refuted the Jews publicly, showing from the Scriptures that Jesus is the Christ"* (20). This means he used Genesis to Malachi. Nothing else! It also means that this mighty man of God recognised the need to be so immersed in God's Word that he knew how to go about evangelism in such a way that he could trace the treasures of Christ in all these books from beginning to end. So he says, *"Preach the word!"* (21). It's the Word of God; preach His Deity. It's the Word of the Lord; preach His authority. It's the Word of Christ; preach His beauty. We need to be so absorbed by it that we preach it. We are evangelists with the Word; we are teachers with the Word; and we are drawing from the Scriptures, no matter whom we are trying to reach and enrich.

The living Word

A gathering of Gideon's was asked if they had ever thought what they were leaving at the bedside in hotel rooms, putting into prisons, or giving to schoolchildren where it's still permitted. The truth is, they are giving:

- a light – Ps.119:105
- a fire – Jer.23:29
- a hammer – Jer.23:29
- water – Eph.5:26
- dew – Deut.32:2
- rain – Deut.32:2
- food – Prov.30:8

While praying in the Upper Room, the Lord Jesus referred to the value of what he spoke into His disciples' lives: *"I have given them Your word"* (22). How will He speak into our lives and into the lives of others without the presentation of God's Word? This book is a builder. Paul says in Acts 20:32, *"I commend you to God and to the word of His grace, which is able to build you up."* We have already seen in the letter to the Hebrews it's also a sword. The Word of God is living and powerful - others versions may say "active" – sharper than any two-edged sword, piercing and dividing. This is the great ministry of the Word.

It's living, which means it is lively. When we read the word "living" in the New Testament, such as having a "living hope," the word can be translated as "lively," and because the Word of God is lively it makes alive and keeps people lively. Look at a Christian who loves the Word of God and you can guarantee that person is lively. But look at believers who are not in the Word and you will be hard-pushed to find evidence of liveliness. We will be like a dimming bulb if we are not often in the Word of God. He says it's lively and powerful – in the Greek language it is the word for energy. The Word of God is energetic and it makes others energetic.

However, we can fail to be lively when we run out of energy; and we get spiritually breathless, because we are not often enough in the Word. It stimulates and triggers in us all the affection that's needed toward God, toward fellow-believers, and toward others who need to be reached for Christ. This same energy also triggers the endeavor, the stewardship that translates inner affection into outward testimony.

A dear old sister in the north of Burma used to walk with the aid of a long pole, as she slowly made her way to the Hall to spend time alone in prayer. Very often, she was first to arrive for a church gathering, coming half an hour before starting-time to spend time in prayer for the meeting. The amazing thing was, she couldn't read, but she was living proof that the Word of God is living, active and sharp. It has an ability to pierce and penetrate deep into parts of our lives that no other book can reach and, no matter what other book we might take from our bookshelves, it will never replace our Bible. It may assist, it may detract, but it will never replace. This is the book, and if we can only love it as we should and let it have its place in our hearts, in the assembly, and in the neighbourhood, what a difference we would make!

Whenever the Word of God comes into our lives, it has the power to observe and comment on whatever we do or whatever we feel. It divides between the thoughts and the intents of the heart. We couldn't put a razor blade between these, but the Word of God fits between them. When thoughts are hatched in the mind, between then and the moment they become intentions, the Word of God wants to come in between, either to blend the two or to keep them apart. This is its ministry, and only through its power can we ever be entitled to say like the Reformers – Sōlā scrīptūrā!

(1) 2 Cor.11:4; Gal.1:6 (2) Rom.1:16 (3) Gen.2:7,8 (4) Isa.43:21; 44:21 (5) Rom.8:29; Phil.3:10,21; Rom.12:2; 2 Cor.3:18 (6) 2 Cor.2:17 (7) Rev.2:9 (8) Rev.3:8 (9) Heb.1:3; Jn 1:1,14 (10) 1 Tim.3:16 (11) 2 Tim.3:16 (12) 2 Pet.1:21 (13) Heb.13:15, RV (14) Matt. 22:23,29 (15) Lk.24:27 (16) Lk.24:32 (17) Acts 20:28, RV (18) 1 Tim.4:13,16 (19) 1 Tim.4:12 (20) Acts 18:28 (21) 2 Tim.4:2 (22) Jn 17:14

Chapter Three: Solus Christus – Christ Alone

So the Bible is infallible, impeccable, reliable, and inerrant. How can we be sure? For one unassailable reason: it's the Word of God, of the Lord, and of Christ, so it bears the hallmark of Their Deity, authority, and character. It speaks, and we are accountable to it. Every believer is, and every unbeliever will be. As for the former, the Scriptures must be open for Spirit-given guidance in their Christian walk; and, as for the latter, the final assize of the great white throne will show that "books were opened" (1) one of which, undoubtedly, will be the Word of God. We have the Lord's own assurance of this for He said, *"He who rejects Me, and does not receive My words, has that which judges him – the word which I have spoken will judge him in the last day"* (2).

This is man's guaranteed ultimate accountability of which Paul says, that God *"has appointed a day on which He will judge the world in righteousness by the Man whom He has ordained. He has given assurance of this to all by raising Him from the dead"* (3). It is inevitable that unbelievers will be answerable to *"that"* and to *"Him"*, to the message and the Man. They may believe that they will never be held accountable, due to not being faced with their sin while they live. Solomon was aware of this sort of attitude when he wrote, *"Because the sentence against an evil work is not executed speedily, therefore the heart of the sons of men is fully set in them to do evil"* (4). The Word of Christ reflects Christ the Word, and its perspicuity will be acknowledged by all men, whether by believers at the judgment seat of Christ or by unbelievers at the great white throne.

As believers, we enjoy reading the Bible, because Christ is in all the Scriptures and we want to see Him. Colossians 2:9-10 sums up all that we are in Him, especially when we see that what Paul says is linked to the last word of verse 8 – "Christ". It is in Him alone – Solus Christus – *"dwells all the fulness of the Godhead bodily; and you are complete in Him."* Chapter 3 begins by lifting our sights: *"If then you were raised with Christ, seek those things which are above, where Christ is, sitting at the right hand of God. Set your mind on things above, not on things on the earth. For you died and your life is hidden with Christ in God. When Christ who is our life appears, then you also will appear with Him in glory."* No wonder we are drawn to the end of verse 11 to confess that we are nothing without Him – *"but Christ is all and in all."*

Have you ever wondered how God felt as He watched the Lord Jesus Christ go to Calvary? He must have been so moved in His own appreciation and evaluation as His Son fulfilled what had been planned from eternity. We also might wonder what He felt when another 33-year-old man left his home bound for the Castle Church with his theses firmly in his grip to nail them to its door. Figuratively speaking we could say that he drove that nail home with five blows:

- Sōlā Scrīptūrā – Scripture alone
- Solus Christus – Christ alone
- Sōlā Grātiā – Grace alone
- Sōlā Fidē – By faith alone; and
- Sōlī Deō Gloria – the glory of God alone

As we have already thought, the reason for the first is to reveal the second, and it's worth noting how Christ-centred the letters to the Philippians and the Colossians are. The name of "Christ" seems to be given special attention, whereas the letter to the Hebrews gives equal attention to His names as Christ and Jesus. It may have been pointed out to us that the disciples never called Him Jesus during their time with Him on earth, that they addressed Him as Lord, and we should do the same. Well, quite evidently, no one mentioned this to the writer of Hebrews for nine times over he refers to Him as "Christ" and another nine times solely to "Jesus" to imprint on the minds of Jewish believers that "Christ" is the Messiah and that "Jesus" is the Son of God. How fitting it is that they should be reminded that this Jesus, rejected by men on the cross, is the same Jesus that God welcomed to His throne as the One in whom God's whole treasury resides! (5).

This was depicted as early as Genesis 25 when Abraham gave all that he had to Isaac (v.5), and we do well to note the timing he chose. In taking Isaac to Moriah, which is the same landscape as Calvary, we can trace the foreshadowing of:

- the death of Christ as our substitute in chapter 22;
- the setting aside of Israel in the death of Sarah, in chapter 23;
- and bringing home a bride for Isaac in chapter 24, just as Christ will welcome His bride at His coming to the air.

It should make us wonder what the conversations were like between Abraham and Isaac after Moriah. Surely, they must have talked about it. Is it really thinkable that Isaac would have come off the altar without feeling the relief or saying to his father, "Were you really going to go through with that?" Abraham gave him all that he had, but it was after Moriah; whereas, it was in the anticipation of the cross that Jesus went up the stairway to the Upper Room knowing that the Father had given all things into his hands (6) – before the cross, and before obtaining His bride. It wasn't done because He had been to Calvary and because the bride had been brought home. No, it was given in the expectation, in the eternal anticipation, that the eternal Son would fulfill the eternal purpose.

The oneness of the Father and the Son

The Lord Jesus could say *"I and My Father are one"* (7) – one in Person, in purpose, and in power. Everything in the Father is in the Son. Whether we think of His communicable attributes or non-communicable attributes, they are all in Christ. *"Of His fullness we have all received"* (8) – that's one of God's communicable attributes through Christ. We have been given faith to believe, forgiveness, and many other things besides, including peace and hope. All these belong to the very nature of God and they're communicable, but in the Lord Jesus there also are attributes that are incommunicable. For example: His deity and eternity, His omniscience, His omnipotence, His self-existence, and His sovereignty. None of these is communicable. We have been made partakers of the divine nature (9), but this doesn't make us equal with deity. Similarly, He came in the likeness of sinful flesh, which didn't give him depravity, so there's a big difference in the way the Lord Jesus came in the body that was prepared for Him without sharing what is wrong in us - for that would have reduced Him to being less than God.

The pleasure of the Father in the Son

"It pleased the Father that in Him all the fullness should dwell" (10). Why? Because He expresses Himself as the image of the invisible God: not merely the visible expression of God, but the image of the invisible God. We could think this means that men might see what God was like, but it may hold a much deeper thought, that He is the full personification of God's invisibility. This means there are things that remained invisible in Him. For example, the glory of God was manifested in the wedding at Cana (11), but not the glory that He had before the world was (12). So there was something very different about Him that allowed His disciples to realise that God meant something more, because He was that in eternity past in His deity before stepping

down to make His deity known in His humanity. Before He had a body, He was the image of the invisible God, and He came down here still baring the image of the invisible God. Yes, it pleased the Father that in Him alone all that fullness would dwell.

In response to this, the Lord Jesus was able to say, *"I always do those things that please Him"* (13). But the pleasure of the Father was reciprocated by the pleasure of the Son. This allows the Lord Jesus always to be viewed by His Father in the words that He used in Matthew 17: *"This is My beloved Son, in whom I am well pleased"* (14). That pleasure has different aspects to it. It was the pleasure of who He is in His eternal nature, His co-equality, even in His manhood, with the Eternal Father. *"Yet it pleased the Lord to bruise Him; He has put Him to grief. When You make His soul an offering for sin, He shall see His seed, He shall prolong His days, and the pleasure of the Lord shall prosper in His hand"* (15).

So the verse that begins with pleasure ends with pleasure, that the pleasure God expressed in the Sacrifice of the cross will be expressed in Him eternally, because God's pleasure rests comfortably in His hand. John 3:35 echoes this for it says, *"The Father loves the Son, and has given all things into His hand."* It's remarkable that the word "hand" is singular here, just as it is in Isaiah 53:10. Why? God is declaring His trust and dependence on the deity and infinite ability of His co-equal Son, and the Old Testament and New Testament confirm this.

As Creator, He *"has measured the waters in the hollow of His hand* [singular], *Measured heaven with a span* [singular]" (16).

As Lord and Saviour, *"All things have been delivered to Me by My Father"* (17) and *"All authority has been given to Me in heaven and on earth"* (18).

As Judge, *"For the Father judges no one, but has committed all judgment to the Son"* (19).

As Heir, *"God ... has in these last days spoken to us by His Son, whom He appointed heir of all things"* (20).

But then we notice a change in the Upper Room:

As Servant, *"Jesus, knowing that the Father had given all things into His hands* [plural], *and that He had come from God and was going to God* (21), anticipated the cross with this pledge, *"I have finished the work which You have given Me to do"* (22).

In His manhood and servanthood, Jesus appreciated what God had given Him; so much that He gripped it with both hands as the humble Servant, knowing that men were about to drive nails through them. This they were able to do, because God permitted them, but they could never remove what inwardly He was holding, and by dying on the cross He proved that the work of redemption was safely in His hands.

The confidence of the Father in the Son

Loving His Son and entrusting Him with so much shows the evaluation that God placed on Christ. Calvary was His way of saying, "Solus Christus – Christ alone." As far as the Father was concerned, there was no alternative – the only begotten from the Father was the only one.

This should be our greatest confidence that helps us to do the same. What better reason could we give than to share the Father's confidence in His Son? We can have confidence, because His Father entrusted so much into the safekeeping of His Son. What, then, will we not entrust to His hands during the crises of our years, when the Father has committed "the eternal purpose which He purposed in Christ Jesus our

Lord"? (23). Putting our needs in His hands is an acknowledgement of His lordship; not putting our needs into His hands reminds us that if He's not Lord of all, He's not Lord at all.

But God ensured that something else happened when the Saviour died. He nailed other things to the cross, things that men could never nail. One was *"the handwriting of requirements that was against us"* (24), the other was our sinful selves. Long before Luther had the idea of nailing something to the church door, God thought of nailing our indebtedness to the Cross along with his Son. The promise made through Isaiah would be fulfilled by Him – *"He will exalt the law and make it honourable"* (25). Only the perfect Law-giver could be the perfect Law-keeper and, by fulfilling the promise in His death as our sin-bearer, He enabled *"the righteous requirement of the law* [to] *be fulfilled in us"* (26). By nailing our debt with Him there, our sinful limitations were overcome, and we resist sin by walking *"according to the Spirit"* (26). In Christ alone, God conquered the law of sin and death and brought us into the freedom of the law of the Spirit of life in Christ Jesus.

Apart from our limitations, our separation from God has been overcome for each believer can say, *"I have been crucified with Christ; it is no longer I who live, but Christ lives in me"* (27). In communion with God, we should cry out, "Solus Christus!" – Christ alone!

It was this in the heart of Martin Luther, who was so tired of the Word of God being corrupted by the Roman system, that all he wanted was to lay hold on its liberating truths in the gospel. Yes, we might wonder how God felt when He saw the dawning of that new day – 31st October 1517, shortly before Luther's 34th birthday – when this young man had the courage to grasp the bull by its horns. He drove the nail home on that door, but to this day it has not conceded the ground that it should have.

Our security in the Son

Being crucified with Christ is how our spiritual journey began, and it's also how it continues. This is the marvel of Colossians chapter 3:1-4. We were *"raised with Him"* (v.1). As soon as we were saved, each of us could have learned to say, "I'm raised together *with* Christ. I'm with him, and can never be separated. I have been made alive and it's impossible to become dead in sin." In Christ we have finished with the idea that we can lose our salvation. To be lost again, we would need to undo all the doctrines of grace. We would need to become un-elected, un-predestined, un-called, un-justified, un-seated, un-forgiven, un-redeemed, un-born, un-glorified, and become un-saved. Oh yes, in Christ we get the point.

We can't ever lose our salvation, because we are hidden with Him. First things first: we were raised *with* Christ, and then we were hidden *in* Christ. "Raised" is how we began, "hidden" is how we continue, and the third is how we will appear *with* Him in glory. When He appears, we also shall appear with Him and be manifested with Him in glory. So the way God began our salvation in Christ is the way He ends – we are always and permanently with Him.

A very dear sister in the Lord was sitting, leaning toward the pew in front of her, with a great smile on her face as she listened to how D.L. Moody had said that Christians are not only going to heaven, they are already in heaven. What we cherish as a future prospect seemed to dawn on her as a joyful, present reality, and she was glad to be given a copy of Moody's book on 'Heaven'. It doesn't make us heavenly though, does it? We are kind of earthly heavenly specimens. However, we are already seated with Him and guaranteed to be heaven-bound.

Resting on the great assurance that, *"There is therefore now no condemnation to those who are in Christ"* (28) we surrender ourselves to Him, knowing that *"what things were gain to me, these I have counted loss for Christ*" (29). In heartfelt appreciation of all He has done, is doing and will do, for us, we consider it an honour to say that we are *in* Christ (30), that we will be *with* Christ (31), and that by living *for* Christ we can say with Paul, *"For to me, to live is Christ"* (32). How did we obtain all this? We obtained it through the Word and through Christ Himself, along with the other features that we will think about in the next three chapters - through redeeming grace, through saving faith, and through God's desire to bring us to glory.

Listen! We can almost hear the hammer blows striking the Castle Church door, reminding us that the beginning of the Reformation was a recovery of something wonderful for us all. If this is what Luther felt as he went back to his home, which still stands in Wittenberg, he must have gone with mixed feelings. In one way, he would have gone with a heavy heart, yet he would put his head on his pillow that night wondering what the response would be. Having had the courage to do what God had asked him to do, he probably rested in the belief that hammering the nail was his work, but that smiting the hearts of the opposers was God's work.

God sent him knowing what the response would be, and this allows us to share the sense of triumph that points backward to the cross and onward to the response He has fixed in our hearts – Solus Christus!

"Faint not nor fear, His arms are near;

He changeth not, and thou art dear;

Only believe, and thou shalt see

That Christ is all in all to thee."

(John S.B. Monsell)

(1) Rev.20:12 (2) Jn 12:48 (3) Acts 17:31; see also Rom.2:16 (4) Eccles.8:11 (5) Col.2:3 (6) Jn 13:3 (7) Jn 10:30 (8) Jn 1:16 (9) 2 Pet.1:3 (10) Col.1:19 (11) Jn 2:11 (12) Jn 17:5 (13) Jn 8:29 (14) Matt.17:5 (15) Isa.53:10 (16) Isa.40:12 (17) Matt.11:27 (18) Matt.28:18 (19) Jn 5:22 (20) Heb.1:1,2 (21) Jn 13:3 (22) Jn 17:4 (23) Eph.3:11 (24) Col.2:14 (25) Isa.42:21 (26) Rom 8:1-4 (27) Gal.2:20 (28) Rom.8:1 (29) Phil.3:7 (30) Phil.1:1 (31) Phil.1:23 (32) Phil.1:21

Chapter Four: Sōlā Grātiā - Grace Alone

It was C.H. Spurgeon, the preacher from the Metropolitan Tabernacle in London, who said, "Repentance was never yet produced in any man's heart apart from the grace of God." So God begins with grace in the experience of sinners, and it's the goodness of God that leads us to repentance. He doesn't take us and wring us out like an old cloth to squeeze repentance from us. No, He deals with us in the kindness of His grace, and repentance flows from the heart of the convicted sinner.

But when was grace first shown? Where did God begin? When Paul wrote in Romans 6:14, "You are not under law but under grace", did he mean that grace began at Pentecost? Thankfully not! There has never been an age without grace. If we go through the ages that can be pinpointed in our Bibles – of innocence in the garden to conscience and government and promise and law and grace and finally the one that's still to come in the thousand-year reign of the Saviour on earth. There is grace in each one of them.

Grace in the old covenant

To answer the question, I can't help but think that it was in the Garden of Eden itself, during the days of unbroken fellowship when God was communing with Adam and Eve. They must have known that He is the God of grace, even when after they sinned He came looking for them. Were they ever in any doubt that He is the God of grace? They didn't go looking for him – no sinner ever does. It's the work of the Spirit of God who begins the process of graciously drawing each of us to Christ. But, for the first time, they also knew the mercy of God for He slew the animal and from its skin He clothed them. He didn't need to do that, but He revealed Himself as the gracious and merciful God. Some have wondered about the difference between grace and mercy and the simplest answer is that grace gives us from God what we do not deserve, and mercy prevents us from getting from God what we do deserve.

So the gracious God was in the Garden of Eden, and it was a gracious God who planned to call Noah and his family into the ark. Genesis chapter 6 comes to the rescue to support the idea that grace didn't begin in a New Testament presentation of the nature of God. When Noah found grace in the eyes of the Lord (1) it was against a background of lawlessness and unrighteousness. Out of the earth's population, whatever its aggregate was at the time, only eight were saved, as God called to Noah, *"Come into the ark, you and all your household"* (2). What an act of divine grace that was, especially since we know that in these post-Adamic days when they were living under *"the law of sin and death"* (Rom.8:2) that they found grace.

Genesis 6 shows that God was still working as he began. Then came the day when Moses went out to the tent he had pitched outside the camp and, whenever he went inside to commune with God, the pillar of cloud came down and stood outside the doorway (3). It was in the enjoyment of this wonderful communion that Moses heard God say something very similar to what He had said to Noah: *"I know you by name, and you have also found grace in My sight"* (4).

When we move on to post-Moses' days, but still under Mosaic law, we read of grace that was expressed to Ezra. Chapter 8 of his book is all about the building work that was underway in Jerusalem after the captivity, when Ezra the marvellous man of God knew what it was to follow Moses' example by bringing the people out to meet God (5). Ezra had a definite purpose in mind when he gathered the people beside the River Ahava: he wanted to see the people of God's decline completely reversed. It wasn't enough for him to see it curtailed, he wanted it removed, so he pleaded with God and all the people fasted and prayed at the riverside. These were days when the adversary had been at work; compromise was everywhere, yet God was at work too. Hard hearts were being softened and turned, and Ezra had the moving experience of leading a time of fasting prayer, and was able to say, *"So we fasted and entreated our God for this, and He answered our prayer"* (6).

A time of brokenness followed, but it was at the expense of deep confession of sin in the following chapter, after the terrible news was passed on that so much inter-marrying had taken place among the nations, not only affecting the people, the priests and Levites, but that the leaders were first in this wholesale downfall. This added to Ezra's burden and He pleaded with God about this too, while admitting that he tore his clothes, plucked out his hair and beard, and was utterly devastated. God's timings are very selective, and we should note that it was at the time of the evening sacrifice that Ezra fell on his knees feeling ashamed and humiliated before God because of *"our iniquities"* and *"our guilt"*. He became so identified with their failure and knew that, although captivity in Babylon was over, the people of God were in captivity to sin in their own land. In the midst of their guilt and grief, and as the desire for a renewed covenant grew in their hearts (7), Ezra must have held dear the assurance he felt in chapter 9:8 – *"And now for a little while grace has been shown from the LORD our God, to leave us a remnant to escape, and to give us a peg in His holy place, that our God may enlighten our eyes and give us a measure of revival in our bondage."*

These are wonderful periods when God's grace was shown, yet the word "grace" is mentioned only twenty times in the whole of the New King James Version of the Old Testament. Thankfully, the coming of the Lord Jesus was a new dawning, and saw the presentation of grace in a way that had never been known before. If the New Covenant would surpass the old, if it were to be better, if its hope better, then the means of obtaining it needed to be better; so God did this by giving the Lord Jesus Christ as a better sacrifice. We would say God gave His best, but, since God compares only the old with the new in the letter to the Hebrews, He speaks only of what is "good" and "better."

When we read what Paul wrote to Titus, we see that he sums up the Lord Jesus by saying, *"The grace of God ... has appeared"* (8). God is the God of all grace – and this tells us there's no other source for it – there's no grace anywhere else outside of Him. Hindu and Buddhist friends refer to the grace of god, but they are not talking about what we are talking about. They use the phrase but they don't know the Person.

Grace in the Person

When the grace of God appeared, it wasn't simply a characteristic that appeared, it was the character, the very embodiment of grace. There were gracious men in the Old Testament – Ruth found grace in the eyes of Boaz, her redeemer (9), Hannah wanted to see grace in Eli (10), her high priest, and David found grace in Jonathan, the king's son (11) – but Jesus is more than a gracious Man, He is grace. Isn't it great that we can look for the grace of God and see it in Him – as our Redeemer, our High Priest, and as the God-given Son? He is the Incarnate God and because He is, for the first time the world saw Incarnate Grace, which makes a huge difference to our understanding of what makes the New Covenant better. In Him dwells all the fulness of the Godhead bodily, and He is full of grace and truth.

This means that grace is always truthful and truth is always gracious. There's a perfect balance in the Lord Jesus that allows Him to be filled with both of these at once. We can't understand this. We can quote the words, yet not know how it is achieved. If a bottle is full of water, it can't also be filled with anything else! But in the Lord Jesus these two glorious truths reside in equal measure; He is full of grace and truth, and much more besides!

Psalm 45 is an invitation to worship, and many have exalted the Lord Jesus Christ by saying, *"I speak the things which I have made touching the King"* (RV). The psalmist then adds, *"grace is poured into Thy lips"* – but from where? Was it from outside or inside? Well, it's obvious that Deity needs no external source of grace, so it's from inside. The One who is full of grace speaks words of grace, and men marvelled at the words of grace that proceeded from his mouth. However, when He said, *"Go, tell that fox"* (12) He was still being gracious. When He called the Pharisees and Sadducees a *"Brood of vipers,"* (13) He was still being gracious. When He told the scribes and Pharisees they were *"hypocrites"* and *"like whitewashed tombs"* (14) He was still being gracious, because He never speaks in any other way. Grace is poured into His lips and He was being truthful and gracious at the same time.

That's a challenge for us to emulate, isn't it? Following Him as our example, we are to speak the truth in love (15) and always with grace (16). How easy it is to dilute grace by saying something that isn't quite truthful! You give someone a compliment and then you go away and admit to yourself that it really wasn't what you think at all. Or you try to act graciously, and then go away thinking, 'Well, if only they knew the truth.' There's never that conflict with the Lord Jesus – grace and truth are always complementary in Him.

Grace in the gospel

When we go through our Bibles, we discover God is well pleased when grace is in the person, but he wants to see it elsewhere. He wants to see it in the preaching, so that whenever we handle the Word of God it is done in the character of Him of whom it speaks. If God is the God of all grace, and He is; if the Lord Jesus Christ was the bodily presentation of grace in this world, and He was; then we must genuinely represent Him in our preaching by speaking words that are grace and truth. *"By grace you are saved through faith,"* (17) combined with *"belief in the truth"* (17) and this is brought about by the work of the Spirit of grace (18) and the Spirit of truth (19). He makes it possible by bringing us to Christ and by Christ bringing us to God. We were reconciled to God through the death of His Son, and the Holy Spirit brought us to Christ through conviction and by leading us to repentance, so the whole Trinity are inseparably bound up in the revelation of grace. Now that's the gospel, the gospel of the grace of God.

"The Gospel of Thy grace

My stubborn heart has won,

For God so loved the world

He gave His only Son,

That whosoever will believe,

Shall everlasting life receive!"

(A.T. Pierson)

It has other names, too. When we read the first two chapters of Romans, we will find three different ways of referring to the gospel. Paul says in verse 1, I'm *"separated to the gospel of God"*: He is the Source of the gospel. In verse 9, it is called *"the gospel of His Son"*: He is the Subject of the gospel. Thirdly, in verse 16, we find that it's also *"the gospel of Christ"*: He is the Centre of the gospel. Finally, when we go into the second chapter, in verse 16, Paul makes it very personal, by saying, it is *"my gospel"*: for he, and we, are the sinners to whom the message is sent. What belongs to God, what belongs to His Son, and what belongs to Christ in the gospel is ours, and we possess it because He made it possible. It's the gospel of the grace of God. We would never have it any other way.

But through the great justifying work of God in Christ, he says *"through whom also we have access by faith into this grace in which we stand"* (20). Right at the moment we were helped by the Spirit of God to exercise faith, God brought us into the grace of the gospel, and we should learn to be immersed in the doctrines of grace. If we are weak in the doctrines of the gospel, in our understanding of its glorious truths, we should immerse ourselves in them. We ought to be familiar with them for they are the lifeblood of the saints. How God saved us really ought to be at the very core of all that we understand in His Word, so that the essential nature of how we live can be more fully understood and appreciated. Otherwise, we will be vague in our service, because we are vague in the doctrines of the gospel.

When we are reading through our New Testament we discover that, if God sees this in the Person of His Son, and He has and does, and also wants to see it in the preaching, then that's going to be achieved by certain means. How does He achieve it? Well, it's no surprise, He does it by His grace! When Luther and the Reformers said, 'Sōlā Grātiā', it covered the whole spectrum from salvation to the glory. They knew it wasn't entered by penance or maintained by indulgences. No, for they knew that we are never going to be without grace from the moment we are saved until the moment He calls us Home to heaven. The wonder is that even then there's more for we *"rest* [our] *hope fully upon the grace that is to be brought to* [us] *at the revelation of Jesus Christ"* (21). It's all embraced in the gospel of the grace of God, so, first of all, it's in the Man, and then it's in the message.

John wrote that it is *"of His fulness we have all received, and grace for grace"* (22), so this is God's provision in the message. The one who gave the message provides for the person who comes to Him, and through the provision we discover the character of grace. Sometimes it's in our difficulties that we discover it, when He says, *"My grace is sufficient for you"* (23), and we know how often it is throughout the course of our lives that the grace of the Lord Jesus has been shown to us in our circumstances. But when we go to the likes of Peter's first epistle and read through the five chapters we discover that grace is varied. He calls it *"manifold grace"* (24), meaning it is variegated: many-faceted or multi-coloured.

You could describe its facets as being sacrificial and eternal in chapter 1, spiritual, moral and practical in chapter 2, marital in chapter 3, Pentecostal in chapter 4, and doctrinal in chapter 5:12 when he says, *"this is the true grace in which you stand."* Everything that's taught in the five chapters is put under this umbrella title of the true grace of God.

As we look at the range of service that we are called to fulfil and see our own personal stewardship within it, we can rightly claim from Ephesians 4:7 that, *"to each one of us grace has been given."* But what is he talking about? He's not thinking of our salvation, but referring to what's included in our service, specifically to the matter of spiritual gifts that we have in Romans 12, 1 Corinthians 12, Ephesians 4 and 1 Peter 4.

He's not speaking solely about saving grace, he's speaking about keeping grace. This is the grace we experience from day to day in our spiritual understanding and application of His Word. For instance, as we discover the requirements of its practicalities during suffering and trial; also in the ups and downs of marital life; and in the fulfilment derived from the spiritual gifts that were introduced at Pentecost. All of this, he says in 1 Peter 5:12, belongs to *"the true grace of God."* So whatever we are going through, and in whatever particular department in which there's need, we know God's grace will provide.

It's as if there's a rainbow in 1 Peter 4 verse 10 that shines in the light of God's Word as its spectrum gets refracted, and we understand that the manifold grace of God is the variety of gifts that are given to those in the church, which is the body of Christ, that they might please God

in their lifetime of service. So it's very important that we understand
our calling: that is, what God has called us to do as well as what He has
called us to be.

Grace in suffering

Finally, we come to what Peter says about suffering in 1 Peter 2:19: *"it
is commendable, if because of conscience toward God one endures grief,
suffering wrongfully."* A very distraught young sister shared details of
her unhappy marriage, and wrote about what she was going through.
In part of her summary, she spoke highly of how God was helping her
to accept it, and I responded saying it was not only acceptable to her, it
was acceptable to God. In fact, it was not only acceptable, He says it was
"commendable," (25) and His word for commendable is the word *charis*
– grace. How comforting and reassuring! Remember, *"It is grace"*, if
because of conscience toward God you are enduring griefs and suffering
wrongfully, and the One who knows all about it enables you to handle
it commendably.

One day, we will look back over our lives at troughs where we were
put to the test, through no fault of our own, and, like this young girl,
something of His grace will emerge as we reflect on how an expression
of His help shone through your tears. Yes, there can be heartache
associated with this grace. "It is the way the Master went, should not
the servant tread it still?" (Horatius Bonar) (26).

Some of God's people are at their wits' end and being helped by His
grace. It's as if they have a special outpouring of grace, so that what
they have found in the Man, in His message, in His character, in His
doctrine, and in His gifts, they also experience in His ministry to them
in their suffering, and they triumph through His grace. It's part of the
outpouring of His fulness that we have all received, and grace for grace.
This is grace upon grace or grace in place of grace: like stones on a

riverbed constantly having today's water following yesterday's, just as the Christian has grace that gives "strength for today and bright hope for tomorrow" (T.O. Chisholm) (27). In Him is all the fulness of grace, and He is constantly pouring it out like Elisha with the pot of oil that filled all the buckets and the basins and the bowls, yet at the end there was still as much in the original container as there was at the beginning (28). Isn't that just like God?

Since coming to Christ, we have found that in our circumstances, as well as in all other aspects of grace, that God is revealing Himself to us in ways that are so meaningful and helpful, and as we recognise this, we sing:

> Jesus, be the centre. Be my source, be my light, Jesus.
>
> Jesus, be the centre. Be my hope, be my song, Jesus.
>
> Be the fire in my heart. Be the wind in these sails,
>
> Be the reason that I live, Jesus.
>
> Jesus, be my vision. Be my path, be my guide, Jesus.
>
> (Vineyard)

"For you know the grace of our Lord Jesus Christ that though He was rich, yet for your sakes He became poor, that you through His poverty might become rich" (29). In the message, in the character, in the doctrine, in the gifts, and then in our suffering, He pours out the riches of His grace. And just as He has done in all these different periods of time from the Garden of Eden to the present day, He will extend it further to post-tribulation days of which He said, *"I will pour out on the house of David and on the inhabitants of Jerusalem the Spirit of grace and supplication; and they shall look on Me whom they pierced. Yes, they will*

mourn for Him as one mourns for his only son, and grieve for Him as one grieves for a firstborn" (30).

Their grief will be the evidence of His grace, a land shall be born in one day, and a nation shall be brought forth at once (31). As Isaiah also said, *"The remnant will return, the remnant of Jacob, to the Mighty God"* (32), and, like all who are redeemed through the precious blood of Christ, they will owe it to – Sōlā Grātiā!

(1) Gen.6:8 (2) Gen.7:1 (3) Ex.33:9 (4) Ex.33:12 (5) Ex.19:17; 29:43 (6) Ezra 8:23 (7) Ezra 10:3 (8) Tit.2:11 (9) Ruth 2:2,10, KJV (10) 1 Sam.1:18, KJV (11) 1 Sam.20:3 KJV (12) Lk.13:32 (13) Matt.3:7 (14) Matt.23:27 (15) Eph.4:15 (16) Col.4:6 (17) Eph.2:8; 2 Thess.2:13 (18) Zech.12:10; Heb.10:29 (19) Jn 16:13 (20) Rom.5:2 (21) 1 Pet.1:13 (22) Jn 1:16 (23) 2 Cor.12:9 (24) 1 Pet.4:10 (25) 1 Pet.2:19 (26) Go Labour On (27) Great is Thy Faithfulness (28) 2 Kin.4:1-7 (29) 2 Cor.8:9 (30) Zech.12:10 (31) Isa.66:8 (32) Isa.10:21

Chapter Five: Sōlā Fidē - By Faith Alone

Building blocks are a good idea. This is true in composition, communication or construction, and there's no doubt that the five Solas are God-given building blocks. The same can be said of an architect's drawing: it describes a plan, defines a planner, delivers a purpose, delights an occupier, and determines an objective. In a similar way through the Scriptures, Christ is made known as Saviour, grace is expressed, faith has a basis, and God will be glorified. Romans chapter 10:17 sums this up perfectly: *"So then faith comes by hearing, and hearing by the word of God,"* and Hebrews 11:1 adds, *"Now faith is the substance of things hoped for, the evidence of things not seen."*

This is contrary to the world's opinion, which says 'seeing is believing'; but, since we walk by faith and not by sight, hearing is believing. it's more than significant that it's in the chapter that catalogues those who lived by faith that God presents Himself as the *"builder and maker"* (1). He is both architect and worker, the infinite mind behind the conception and the energy behind the construction. He is designer and deliverer, source and supplier, and the One whose inspired Word instils confidence and undergirds our faith. If faith comes by hearing, and hearing comes by the Word of God, then this Book must be utterly dependable and completely trustworthy.

In his day, no one knew this better than Martin Luther. On the 31st October 1517, he was a man who was totally absorbed by Romans 1:17, *"The just shall live by faith."* It consumed him. Having been immersed in a system of religion that was works-based, he looked at all the indulgences and became convicted by the Spirit of God that Romans 1:17 was the only way of escape for a spiritually imprisoned man. It's not possible to stress to what extent he and his fellow-believers had been captives of a crippled church system, but he was utterly convinced that he could turn to this Book, to such a verse as *"The just shall live by faith",* and ably set out how God developed this wonderful truth. He could see that the first two words, "the just", were developed in the letter to the Romans; that the next two words, "shall live", were developed in the letter to the Galatians; and, finally, he rejoiced in how the last two words, "by faith", are developed in the letter to the Hebrews. So three whole letters came alongside his initial conviction that the just shall live by faith.

What better evidence could there have been that the Spirit of God was moving in him; not only causing him to enjoy a single verse, but to see how the Word of God in its entirety supported it? Just as faith is the support substance of things hoped for, Luther discovered that the Word of God essentially and irreplaceably underpinned the beliefs of which he had become so convicted and convinced.

Living in faith

Let's follow this through for a moment. Each born-again believer is eternally blessed in a God-given sequence. Faith is the substance, the bedrock, the sub-strata of all our hopes; yet it in itself needs to be upheld. So faith lies beneath our hopes, the Word lies beneath our faith, and God Himself is under it all. What a series of gifts! First of all, He has given us Christ, His Son, then through His Spirit He has given us His Word, and through His Word He has given us faith. How well Romans 5:1,2 gathers our blessings, as if God put all five Solas into two verses, to tell us that through faith we have been justified, have access into this grace in which we stand, and that we rejoice in hope of the glory of God.

The Word of God proves this. Peter describes the hope that was given to us at the beginning of our spiritual journey as *"living"* (2) and Paul reminds us that we are walking toward and waiting for the end of the journey with a *"blessed hope"* (3). He also says we have a *"good hope"* (4) that affects us daily in our word and work. We are reminded in Hebrews that we have a *"better hope"* (5), and the writer links it to our service in worship through the Lord Jesus Christ as Priest. Peter expands on this (6), and enlarges our appreciation of the Lord's graciousness by coming continually as worshippers to offer up spiritual sacrifices through Him to God. It's interesting to note how these are reflected in chapter 11's gallery of faith in Abel's worship, Enoch's walk, and Noah's word and work (7), stirring us as present-day believers to enjoy all these aspects of spiritual reality. We can summarise these as follows:

REF.	HOPE	ACTION	O.T.
Heb.7:19	Better	Worship	Abel
Tit.2:12,13	Blessed	Walk & Waiting	Enoch
2 Thess.2:17	Good	Word & Work	Noah

When Paul opened his letter to Titus, he first spoke of *"the faith of God's elect"* (8) before referring *to "common faith"* (9) which emphasised the shared faith they possessed in salvation and were called to express in service. This was expected to affect their walk, and it was for this reason he urged them about *"denying ungodliness and worldly lusts."* So common faith should result in a common walk. Isn't it thrilling to see how one portion of God's Word sheds further light on the initial glimpse that we had of His purpose through men like Abel, Enoch and Noah?

Proof of faith

Yes, faith is the substance of things hoped for, but it also is the evidence of things not seen. Making a profession of faith is one thing, but showing the accompanying proof confirms its reality. How relevant it is that James should write, *"I will show you my faith by my works"* (10). There's an outstanding example of this during the days of Elisha, when the word of the LORD came through him in a time of drought saying, *"Make this valley full of trenches"* (11). Digging is what we could call evidence of the preparation of faith, and visible trenches showed the anticipation of faith when there wasn't a drop of water to be seen. But who was to see the evidence? Was it God? No, for He saw Elisha's faith before he made the announcement; and He saw the people's faith before they started to dig. So who saw it?

Firstly, they saw the expectation of faith in each other; and then the unbelieving enemy saw evidence of the triumph of faith. God's timing was significant for the water came *"in the morning, about the time of offering the oblation"* (12), which coincided with the morning lamb being placed on the altar (13) to prefigure the Lord being put on the Cross at nine o'clock in the morning, through whom we are able to say, *"This is the victory that has overcome the world – our faith"* (14).

It's the working of faith that defines the life and liveliness of the believer. We can't worship without faith, we can't walk without faith and we can't work without faith, so the principles of Genesis come the whole way through New Testament teaching to show that what was applicable back then is applicable to our spiritual experience now. The beauty of it is, that having outlined what pleased Him in these early days of the law of faith, God brings their example forward to these days in which we enjoy the law of the Spirit of life in Christ Jesus, that we may recapture something of what the Reformers felt when they exclaimed, 'Sōlā fidē' – by faith alone.

Challenges to faith

The Lord Jesus Christ gave three particular challenges to His disciples. One of them was, *"Why are you fearful, O you of little faith?"* (15). He could hardly have been more to the point. "Why are you timid?" or, even more critically, "Why are you being cowardly?" In a time of danger when they were being put to the test, when things were hard to take and even harder to understand, the Lord Jesus brought them back to the principle of faith. He knew that in times of danger it was their faith that was endangered. It wasn't just the circumstances; it was their faith, and what happens to it under the circumstances. We can look at our circumstances and begin to wonder if our faith is being undermined or undergirded in our circumstances?

On another occasion He was equally straightforward: *"Oh you of little faith, why did you doubt?"* (16). The first objection was fear, and the second objection was doubt, and both are the enemies of faith. When He asked the question, they were in a little boat on the Lake of Galilee that looked as if was about to sink. It happened on two different occasions: once when Jesus was in the boat, the other when He was not in the boat - and their reactions were equally fearful. Does it not make you wonder if you are as fearful when you are conscious that the Lord is on board with you as you are when you have lost the sense of His being on board?

Oh, we can look at these dear men in the boat and ask the same question. "Why did you doubt?" Why did you waver in your mind? Why did you reach the stage where you had to think twice about things? But their lesson is our lesson. Doubt is still an enemy of faith. Don't we also think twice, at times? Faith needs us to think only once. If faith is the foundation of things hoped for, the things that are to be feared don't have a foundation. We know how easily we give in to fear and lose the sense of the foundation of faith. In this sense, we are all in the same boat.

When the Lord Jesus challenged Peter as he began to sink, He did a remarkable thing. He took hold of him by the hand before asking the same question. It's one of the loveliest moments in the gospels. A man's faith was sinking with him, and the Lord Jesus let him know that He is the Author and Finisher of faith. Christian, always remember that He is holding onto you even when you don't feel that you're holding on to faith. Doubt is a very serious thing. The old maxim is still good advice, "Believe your beliefs and doubt your doubts, otherwise you may end up doubting your beliefs and believing your doubts."

On the third occasion the Lord Jesus asked, *"O you of little faith, why did you reason among yourselves?"* It's not that the Lord expects us to be unreasoning, but there are times when faith should be propping us up and be so satisfying that we don't need to reason any further. We have reached a conclusion in our spiritual understanding of the situation, and faith's ongoing support is part of the *"all things"* (17) that have been given to us freely in Him. But there's another vital lesson here. This wasn't an individual who was being challenged, as Peter was; this was a whole group. It was a collective lack of faith and collective reasoning. To borrow from Peter's experience in chapter 14, they were sinking as a group and needed the Lord to reach out and catch them. We know what it is to face times when we feel ourselves sinking individually, but are there also times when we feel we are sinking as a group, even as an assembly? If Peter's response was, *"Lord, save me!"* the assembly's cry needs to be, "Lord, save us!"

Disputing of faith

Sometimes things happen and we can't figure out 'why?' until we realise that there's some sort of dispute going. Is that not right? There are two good examples of this in the Gospels: one, when the Lord Jesus was walking with His disciples (18); the other while sitting with them in the Upper Room (19). We don't know whether He was behind them or in front as they walked, it makes no difference for He knows all things. However, we can assume they thought they were out of earshot and that He would think they were simply chit-chatting among themselves.

What a shock it must have been when He said, *"What was it you disputed among yourselves on the road?"* (20). They had been trying to decide who was greater among them while they were walking with Him – and worse still when they were sitting with Him when He had just instituted the Lord's Supper – and all that bothered them was 'Are you less than I am?' or 'Am I greater than you are?'

The Greatest was listening on both occasions, so it mattered little if anyone was greater among them. Here again, faith should have come in to cut away the potential of that kind of talk among them. Oh, without a doubt, He could have given the answer for He knew who loved Him most, who was most humble, and who had most faith. Rank was of no importance, and He knew that Peter would get it right when he later wrote to a number of churches and took his place as *"I who am a fellow elder"* (21) among the shepherds of the flock.

Of course, it can be a good sign when someone feels the need to dispute or deliberate. Mary did, when Gabriel came to her and spoke of her being *"highly favoured"* and *"blessed among women"*. Luke says, *"she was troubled"* as she *"considered* (Gr. *dielogizeto) what manner of greeting this was"* (22). In contrast to the mindset of the disciples' dispute, Mary's dialogue with herself was because the lowliness of her mind was overwhelmed by the loftiness of his greeting, yet the greatness of her faith allowed her to grasp that anything "highly" attributed to her was because God had *"regarded the lowly state of His maidservant"* (23). Yes, her whole being was shaken, but her faith wasn't, and she accepted that being "favoured" (Gr. *kecharitōmenē*) meant she was the object of His grace. Sōlā grātiā was wonderfully combined with Sōlā fidē!

In that unique and priceless moment, Mary's faith upheld her acceptance that the incarnation of the Son of God into humanity had been presented to her, and would be fulfilled through her. So we readily understand that her dispute was of a very different kind from that of the disciples, and that its character should be reflected in all our consideration of whatever God reveals to us. At no point was she in disagreement with the will of God, which brings us to the point of thinking about our response to the Solas of the Reformation. We need to see that faith alone means it has to be mine alone. It has to be personal and real. Brothers and sisters, it's then and only then, we can ask ourselves, "What am I doing with the faith that was given to me when I trusted in the Lord Jesus Christ as my Lord and Saviour?"

Possessing faith

It's one thing to think about the contrast between "great faith" and "little faith" (24) (Matt.8:10, 26), quite another to come to terms with the blessings and obligations that belong to what the Scriptures call *"your faith"* (24). What did the Lord Jesus mean when He told the woman who touched the hem of His garments, *"your faith has made you well"*? In what sense was it her faith? I believe he meant it was hers by possession, not by production. In the same way, believers in the Lord Jesus Christ have it, yet we didn't produce it. Your faith allows you to say, "Jesus is mine", just as you can say "my gospel" – both are yours by possession, not by production! In her case, the Lord indicated a pre-existing faith in God being lived out under the law, and therefore was able to address her as "Daughter" through a pre-existing relationship with God.

During the years of the Lord's ministry, a man sat begging outside the temple, probably even on the day of His crucifixion when Jerusalem's crowds were much bigger because of the Passover. Did he hear the commotion of the throng that took Him to Calvary? Did he wonder at the sudden midday darkness? How could he have missed it all, since he was *"laid daily at the gate of the temple"* (25). Fifty days later, he was still there when the city heaved again with residents and visitors on the Day of Pentecost, and it was shortly after that when he had the life-changing experience with Peter and John. It was only then, *"through faith in His name,"* (26) that the accusation above the cross became an assurance in his heart when Peter said, "In the name of Jesus Christ of Nazareth, rise and walk."

Listen to Peter as he continued to challenge the people's amazement: *"Yes, the faith that comes through Him has given this perfect soundness in the presence of you all."* It was 'Sōlā fidē' – faith alone. The man knew the substance, and the people saw the evidence, and long before Hebrews 11:1 was written, he proved it to be true. Peter and John had no gold, but the man also showed, long before Peter would write it, that the *"proof of* [his] *faith"* was *"more precious than gold"* (27). But what was "the proof" of his faith?

Firstly, it was seen by the change in what he was. His cripple days were over. Secondly, it was seen in what he did for he went *"walking, leaping, and praising God."* He didn't go rushing home. No, instead of being an outsider at the gate of the temple, he rushed farther in to acknowledge a work of God. His walk began with worship, and once again we see the consistency of this reasoning, that when God wants to trigger worship in the life of the believer He produces it by faith. God produced it, the man possessed it – the faith which comes through Christ, and from no other source – Sōlā fidē in Solus Christus.

Faith is a gift, and Paul reminds us that, *"to you it has been granted on behalf of Christ, not only to believe in Him, but also to suffer for His sake"* (28). Peter is in full agreement when he includes us among *"those who have obtained like precious faith,"* (29) and we are left to conclude that faith is never attained, but obtained. Friend, God gave it to you freely in Christ. It is His gift, and "your faith"!

Rich in faith

James, the Lord's brother, asked a very important question in James 2:5: *"Has God not chosen the poor of this world to be rich in faith?"* Go among our Christian brothers and sisters in the Chin Hills of Northern Burma and the villages of India, and you will see the proof of this. You will meet God's chosen and see their poverty, but you also will see that God has chosen them to be rich in faith. There they are, *"as unknown, and yet well known ... as sorrowful, yet always rejoicing; as poor, yet making many rich; as having nothing, yet possessing all things"* (30). But is it not true that every believer is rich in faith when God has given us so much in His Son? In one sense, definitely for we are:

- Purified by faith – Acts 15:9
- Sanctified by faith – Acts 26:18
- Propitiation through faith – Rom.3:25
- Justified by faith – Rom.3:28
- Access by faith – Rom.5:2
- Stand by faith – Rom.11:20
- Walk by faith – 2 Cor.5:7
- Live by faith – Gal.2:20
- Received the Spirit through faith – Gal.3:14
- Sons of God through faith – Gal.3:26

- Christ in your heart through faith – Eph.3:17
- Righteousness by faith – Phil.3:9
- Raised through faith – Col.2:12
- Salvation through faith – 2 Tim.3:15
- Understanding by faith – Heb.11:3
- Kept through faith - 1 Pet.1:5

In another sense, we may have to admit, "Definitely not!" for it has been one thing to trust Him for eternity, yet quite another matter altogether to be trusting Him for today. Solomon's greatest song asks, "Who is this coming up from the wilderness, leaning upon her beloved?" She was utterly dependent on him just as we are on the Lord, and it's in the genuineness of our faith that we are leaning upon Him.

"I leave it all with Jesus day by day;

Faith can firmly trust Him, come what may.

Hope has dropped her anchor, found her rest

In the calm, sure haven of His breast;

Love esteems it Heaven to abide

At His side."

(Ellen H. Willis)

The Reformers had it right, and so should we – *Sōlā fidē*.

(1) Heb.11:10 (2) 1 Pet.1:3 (3) Tit.2:12,13 (4) 2 Thess.2:16,17 (5) Heb.7:19 (6) 1 Pet.2:3-5 (7) Heb.11:4-7 (8) Tit.1:1 (9) Tit.1:4 (10) Jas.2:18 (11) 2 Kin.3:16, RV (12) 2 Kin.3:20, RV (13) Ex.29:39 (14) 1 Jn 5:4 (15) Matt.8:26 (16) Matt.14:31 (17) Rom.8:32 (18) Matt.16:8 (19) Lk.22:24 (20) Mk.9:33 (21) 1 Pet.5:1 (22) Lk.1:28,29 (23)

Lk.1:48 (24) Matt.9:22,29 (25) Acts 3:2 (26) Acts 3:16 (27) 1 Pet.1:7,
RV (28) Phil.1:29 (29) 2 Pet.1:1 (30) 2 Cor 6:9,10

Chapter Six: Solī Deō Gloria – The Glory of God Alone

This is the crescendo. All other Solas come from it, and each one exalts it. The Scriptures both reveal His glory and point us to it; Christ ever will be the manifestation of His glory, and He brings us to it (1); grace was brought to us in the glory of the incarnate Person, and we are accepted in Him, our Beloved, *"to the praise of the glory of His grace"* (2), while faith is designed, so that like Abraham we will be *"strengthened in faith, giving glory to God"* (3).

Solomon tells us in his Proverbs that *"It is the glory of God to conceal a matter"* (Prov.25:2), which means he was thinking about the splendour of God and the honour that belongs to His Being. The thought of glory in Hebrew describes it as being a weight or weightiness, so Solomon could easily have been describing the contents of Paul's letter to the Romans. As we know, it contains a wealth of gospel teaching that shows the weightiness of God's reasoning, the weightiness of His revelation, the weightiness of His righteousness combined with every other attribute that is His, until we are overwhelmed by the weightiness of God and an enriching sense of His glory.

This is what we are able to enjoy now, but what about the day when we will experience *"an eternal weight of glory"*? (4) When Solomon referred to God, he was well aware that He is a triune Person; he used the word Elohim, the plural Name of Father, Son and Holy Spirit. He had every right to say "Elohim", of course, because the Father, Son and Holy Spirit are all "of glory", and we know Them as *"the Father of glory"*, *"the Lord of glory"* and *"the Spirit of glory"* (5).

The concealed glory revealed

He was thinking about the triune God having a matter, which really means a word or a message, so he was thinking about the revelation of God and of how He is glorified, even when He conceals His revelation. We know this was true in the Lord's ministry on earth when He chose to speak in parables. As you will recall, the disciples asked Him, *"Why do You speak to them in parables?" He answered and said to them, "Because it has been given to you to know the mysteries of the kingdom of heaven, but to them it has not been given"* (6). So He was glorified both by revealing and concealing. Now if it's the glory of God to conceal it, what we can say when He chooses to reveal it? Solomon's Proverbs could be called Solomon's Parables for that's what the Hebrew words mishlēy Shelomoh mean, and, like the Lord's parables, through them great truths were either hidden or revealed. How do we respond to being on the receiving end of His divine disclosure?

The letter to the Romans is a tremendous revelation in connection with the nature of God, the incarnation of Christ, and the glory of the gospel, so we can well understand why Luther and others focused on the glory of God being sufficient. When they thought of the five Solas, they knew that their high objective and finality rested immovably in Solī Deō Gloria– the glory of God. But it wasn't their idea. They learned it from God Himself, and this is what nerved their convictions and actions. As we do, they saw how He twice emphasised this in Paul's letter. We see it first in the wonderful doxology in the last verse of chapter 11 – *"For of Him and through Him and to Him are all things, to whom be glory forever. Amen."* Five chapters later, and in its final verse, the Spirit of God again leads up to the anthem of praise, that our concluding thought in such undeserved revelation might be, *"To God, alone wise, be glory through Jesus Christ forever. Amen."*

So what did the apostle Paul have in mind when he wrote about the glory of God? The first thing we notice is the timing of the first doxology at the end of eleven chapters of precious gospel revelation. He has taken us from the glory of the incorruptible God in chapter 1:23 and expounded Him and things that are from Him. In a marvellous way, he goes through things in connection with creation, and after stating that we "fall short" of the glory of God, meaning we are completely destitute of it, he links us with justification, redemption, propitiation, regeneration, sanctification, election, predestination, and glorification. At the end of putting all these together, he concludes what we have in these eleven chapters by saying, *"For of Him and through Him and to Him are all things, to whom be glory forever. Amen."*

Christian, these eleven chapters are yours. As you say "Amen" to them and rejoice in the doctrines of grace that are outlined, do you really see the glory of God in them? Is it true that whenever you think about your former depravity you worship Him for bringing you back in touch with His incorruptible glory? (7) When you think of the wonders of creation, does being His new creation make you think of it and be absorbed by His glory or is it enough for you to be absorbed by arguments about it? The same can apply when we take the doctrine of election, for example, and are likely to get caught up in a similar kind of debate. Sometimes, Arminian points of view come along to contradict everything that belongs to the doctrine of election, and vice versa, and we become like the disciples disputing on the road. Oh, the truth of God is worthy of our lowliest mind and highest praise!

In our different understandings of certain teachings of the Word of God, we can be more absorbed in the greater intellect or the greater insight and lose the vision of the greater glory. These doctrines have glory at their very heart, because they come from His heart. They are like the threads of different colours in Aaron's priestly garments: a filament of pure gold was spun into each one. The Spirit of God emphasises that it was "in" the blue, "and in" the purple, "and in" the scarlet, "and in" the fine linen (Ex.39:3).

Just like each of these colours, each precious gospel truth bears the splendour of God's glory. We may not understand everything about creation. We may not understand everything about election, and we never will this side of heaven. Its concept belongs to an infinite mind whose thoughts are higher than our own (8), and we should be thankful that our tiny minds can't resolve its mystery. We don't understand everything about incarnation, justification or redemption, and we don't have so much argument over these, yet they come from the glorious heart of the same glorious God.

When the God of glory appeared to Abraham in Ur of the Chaldees and called him out from that place to learn more and more about the glory of God, he went not knowing where he was going. On the way, he built altars, going step by step with God, and showing it was for Solī Deō Gloria, the glory of God alone. Why? Because even what he didn't know caused him to worship, and this should be our highest response to the truth God shares with us.

The glory of the Son

How has God expressed himself? He has made Himself known first of all through the glory of the Person of His Son, and this is how Paul completed his message to the Romans when he said, *"To God, alone wise, be glory through Jesus Christ forever. Amen."* We will notice a distinct change in the letter at the beginning of chapter 12, where Paul launched into saying, *"I beseech you therefore, brethren, by the mercies of God; that you present your bodies a living sacrifice."* But what did he mean by "therefore"? It's good advice that whenever we see the word "therefore", we should ask 'what it's there for?' It's important to know that the "therefore" which belongs to the presentation of our bodies as living sacrifices has to do with our appreciation and the application of the doctrines of the gospel that are revealed in the first 11 chapters. In other words, we say "Amen" to all that has been taught in them by the God of redemption through the living sacrifice of His Son, and then in consecration offer ourselves as the living sacrifice of His servants.

In the first section Paul speaks about the glory of God at different times. For instance, in chapter 5:2, he attaches the guaranteed hope of the glory of God to the access we have by faith into the grace in which we stand through the gospel. Toward the end of the second section, he applies it in a practical sense in chapter 15:7 by saying, *"Therefore receive one another, just as Christ received us, to the glory of God."* Welcoming one another, and accepting one another, should be a reflection of how Christ has accepted us, which He did to the glory of God. What God expressed by accepting us means that glory is going back to Him through the Lord Jesus Christ, because that's the way it came out to us.

When the disciples saw Him they said, *"We beheld His glory"* (9), and now He wants to see something of it in us. Therefore we take the blessings of the first eleven chapters as our spiritual impetus to fulfil the remaining five with the desire to say, *"To God, alone wise, be glory through Jesus Christ forever. Amen."*

When the disciples looked at the Saviour, they could say they saw His glory. If only this always was our motive in looking to Him! It's possible, however, that we look at the Lord Jesus with the intention of seeing something else instead, something that might glorify us. Some look for prosperity, believing that the gospel is a promissory note for riches, as if faith in Christ is some sort of currency exchange. Others hunger for power that might glorify their so-called 'gift', yet, as Christians, we should have the clearest understanding that all His gifts are intended to glorify the Giver and not the gifted! God invites us to focus on the Lord's glory: firstly, in who He is and what He does, and then in what He has done for us and is doing through us. In the first chapter of John's gospel, the disciple saw the glory of who He is; in the second chapter they saw His glory in what He does.

The second chapter opens with Jesus manifesting His glory by changing water into wine at the wedding in Cana of Galilee, so the glory of the Man was seen in the glory of His ministry in vessels that were filled to the brim. We might have thought it was a manifestation of His power and ability, and there's no doubt it was, but God describes it as a presentation of the glory of who the Saviour is rather than a display of what He can do. This is still His aim in vessels that are filled to the brim.

It's surprising to read that the disciples fell asleep on the Mount of Transfiguration and almost missed seeing His glory, just as they did in Gethsemane when they failed to see Him in His grief. But then Luke goes on to say, *"and when they were fully awake, they saw His glory"* (10). His glory was seen by men who were "fully awake", not half asleep; and in vessels that were full, not half-empty. The wedding and the Mount certainly give lessons that are vital for our Christian walk: we need to be awake to the glory of the Lord, and be vessels that are both filled and ready.

The Lord Jesus is described in Hebrews 1:3 as the outshining of God's glory, and the very image of his Person. All the substance that belongs to Deity resides in Him as *"the fullness of the Godhead bodily"* (11). He lost nothing by coming to earth, except for laying aside the glory that was His prior to His incarnation, which men would have been unable to absorb had He walked among them in the glory that He had in the presence of His Father. Only when the work of the Cross was over did He go home in anticipation of being glorified with the glory that He had with Him before He came (12).

The glory of salvation

God's glory is, first of all, in the Saviour. Secondly, He shows it in salvation. In His pleasure, He has given us the message of which He says is *"the light of the gospel of the glory of Christ"* (13). We have already thought of it in chapter 3 as the gospel of God, the gospel of His Son, the gospel of Christ, and as my gospel, but now God speaks of it as the good news that radiates the glory of Christ. It pleases Him that the eternal glory of the Person shines through His pleasure in the message. Yes, it's the glory of God to conceal a matter, but now we can see His glory revealed in the matter of the Gospel message. It's there to be seen, so it doesn't pay us to be vague in our understanding of the gospel or to be indifferent to its doctrines.

Some have said, "Don't give me doctrine." Really? Everything we know is doctrine. The nature of God is shared with us as doctrine, and our greatest desire should be to learn His attributes. The nature of the gospel is doctrine, and it's there to be enjoyed because by faith we see the glory. The glory of the gospel is wonderful to see and Paul says in 2 Cor.4:6 it is *"the light of the knowledge of the glory of God in the face of Jesus Christ."* How blessed we are that the nature of the invisible God is seen in the face of His Son who says, *"He who has seen Me has seen the Father"* (14). When we see something of the glory of the Lord Jesus through the glory of the gospel we are viewing something of the glory of God.

In Romans 9:23, Paul takes up the thought of believers being vessels of mercy to whom, and through whom, God wants to show the riches of his glory. As part of this glorious gospel of the happy God (15), the One who chose us in Christ before the foundation of the world (16) also prepared us beforehand for glory. Since such revelation comes from the happiness of God, should our happiness not return to Him for bringing us into the blessing of it? Oh, wonder of wonders! It's in the Scriptures alone, ours through Christ alone, revealed through grace alone, enjoyed by faith alone, and all for the glory of God alone!

The glory of eternity

Thirdly, the glory of God is in His intention, and the centre of His purpose, to call us to *"His eternal glory"* (17). We probably didn't know that at the moment we were saved, but isn't it wonderful later to discover that when He called you to salvation, right at that moment He was calling you to eternal glory? There's no hyphen of uncertainty in between. There's no possibility of the first bit failing and the second bit disappearing. You are called, beloved, and preserved (18), and are destined for eternal glory. He guarantees it. Through the gospel, God brings us as *"sons to glory"* (19); during our lives, He helps us grow from *"glory to glory"* (20), and Romans 8:18 tells us, when the sufferings of the present time are over, that further glory will be revealed, not only to us, but *"in us."*

We are going Home to greater glory. In this sense, the glory of God is like the grace of God: it's endless; it's eternal. Paul says that God has called us *"for the obtaining of the glory of our Lord Jesus Christ"* (21). He could have said "to the obtaining of the glory of heaven," and we would have been perfectly satisfied, but he didn't. Has He called us to that place? Very definitely, but better still He has called us to the glory of the Person, and we wait for Him in the reality of that call.

The glory that transforms

In the meantime, God helping us, we continue to love and trust and walk and grow. The more we are in touch with the Lord and His Word, the more we absorb, or should absorb, of the glory of God. Is this not what the Scriptures teach? Listen again, as Paul says, *"But we all, with unveiled face, beholding as in a mirror the glory of the Lord, are being transformed."* Some versions speak of reflecting (22) as in a mirror. However, it's preferable to think of beholding as in a mirror as really speaking about the glory of Christ in the gospel, the glory of the New Covenant, and the glory of the ministry of the Spirit that's revealed in 2 Corinthians 3.

Beholding that glory will transform from one degree of glory to another by the Spirit of the Lord. It's the ongoing process of increasing glory, but we don't get it without being increasingly in the Word. We may wonder why some Christians don't grow. It's because they don't spend enough time with the Lord and His Word. We may also wonder why they don't glow. It's for the same reason. Brothers and sisters, we should ask ourselves how it is that we can claim to walk with the God of light and glory and not be enlightened? How can we walk with Him and not be illuminated?

It was what Martin Luther saw in the teaching of the Roman Catholic Church that made him and others speak about the need for reformation. They saw what was deformed and needed reformed, and it's exactly like that with us. If there is something that's deformed in you, let it be reformed. If there's something in any of the churches that's deformed, let it also be reformed. This is the kind of conviction that forms reforming pioneers and keeps us from being deformed passengers. Like Moses, we need to begin by asking the Lord, *"show me now Your way"*, and continue by adding, *"Please, show me Your glory"* (23) His response will be as Paul expressed it, *"He would grant you, according to the riches of His glory, to be strengthened with might through His Spirit in the inner man"* (24).

How do we get strengthened? By asking for power? No: it's by asking the Lord, "Please, show me Your glory." This is what Paul was outlining for us. It's according to the riches of His glory. That's the secret, and it happens in the inner man as he waits prayerfully in the secret place.

Peter says that *"the Spirit of glory ... rests upon you,"* (25) and He wants to demonstrate this through your life. It's tremendous, isn't it?

"Amazing truth! Tremendous thought!

The Mighty God needs me, e'en me:

My power of limb, my will, my thought;

My individuality.

He asks me for the life He bought,

Amazing truth! Tremendous thought!"

(Anon.)

The glory of the Lamb

As we look to the future, Revelation 21:23 depicts the New Jerusalem that has *"no need of the sun or of the moon to shine in it, for the glory of God illuminated it. The Lamb is its light."* It's described as a cubic city, which, borrowing the symbolism of the Most Holy Place in the Old Testament's tabernacle and temple, represents the perfect holiness of God. Some versions say, *"the Lamb is the light"*, but *"the Lamb is the lamp"* is a better translation of the Greek word *luchnos*. It's a very interesting word, because it means a portable lamp – a light that has moved. In the accuracy and beauty of inspiration, the phrase "the glory of God illuminated it" actually pinpoints when God and the Lamb entered the city to lighten it.

Isn't God's description of the Saviour so wonderful? Presently, He is *"the light of the world"* (26), but in that day He will be the lamp of the city. And we will enter into it to know, at last, what Paul had in mind when he spoke of *"the glory which shall be revealed in us."* We are going to see it, because we are going to see Him in His glory. We have never yet seen Him in His splendour, but glorified bodies will allow us to see Him in a way that faith has never seen Him before. We will be in the presence of God and the Lord Jesus Christ whom not having seen at present we have learned to love (27). What a glorious consideration, and over it all we want to write more indelibly than ever the glory of God alone – *Solī Deō Gloria!*

"He and I in that bright glory

One deep joy shall share –

Mine to be for ever with Him,

His that I am there."

(Mrs Bevan)

(1) Heb.2:10 (2) Eph.1:6 (3) Rom.4:20 (4) 2 Cor.4:17 (5) Eph.1:17; 1 Cor.2:8; 1 Pet. 4:14 (6) Matt.13:10,11 (7) Rom.1:23 (8) Isa.55:8 (9) Jn 1:14 (10) Lk.9:32 (11) Col.2:9 (12) Jn 17:5 (13) 2 Cor.4:4 (14) Jn 14:9 (15) 1 Tim.1:11 (16) Eph.1:4 (17) 1 Pet.5:10 (18) Jude 1 (19) Heb.2:10 (20) 2 Cor.3:18 (21) 2 Thess.2:14 (22) NIV & NRSV (23) Ex.33:13, 18 (24) Eph.3:16 (25) 1 Pet.4:14 (26) Jn 8:12 (27) 1 Pet.1:7.

Appendix 1: The Ninety-five Theses by Luther

Out of love for the truth and from desire to elucidate it, the Reverend Father Martin Luther, Master of Arts and Sacred Theology, and ordinary lecturer therein at Wittenberg, intends to defend the following statements and to dispute on them in that place. Therefore he asks that those who cannot be present and dispute with him orally shall do so in their absence by letter. In the name of our Lord Jesus Christ, Amen.

1. When our Lord and Master Jesus Christ said, "Repent" (Matt.4:17), he willed the entire life of believers to be one of repentance.
2. This word cannot be understood as referring to the sacrament of penance, that is, confession and satisfaction, as administered by the clergy.
3. Yet it does not mean solely inner repentance; such inner repentance is worthless unless it produces various outward mortification of the flesh.
4. The penalty of sin remains as long as the hatred of self (that is, true inner repentance), namely till our entrance into the kingdom of heaven.
5. The pope neither desires nor is able to remit any penalties except those imposed by his own authority or that of the canons.
6. The pope cannot remit any guilt, except by declaring and showing that it has been remitted by God; or, to be sure, by remitting guilt in cases reserved to his judgment. If his right to grant remission in these cases were disregarded, the guilt would certainly remain unforgiven.
7. God remits guilt to no one unless at the same time he humbles

him in all things and makes him submissive to the vicar, the priest.

8. The penitential canons are imposed only on the living, and, according to the canons themselves, nothing should be imposed on the dying.

9. Therefore the Holy Spirit through the pope is kind to us insofar as the pope in his decrees always makes exception of the article of death and of necessity.

10. Those priests act ignorantly and wickedly who, in the case of the dying, reserve canonical penalties for purgatory.

11. Those tares of changing the canonical penalty to the penalty of purgatory were evidently sown while the bishops slept (Matt.13:25).

12. In former times canonical penalties were imposed, not after, but before absolution, as tests of true contrition.

13. The dying are freed by death from all penalties, are already dead as far as the canon laws are concerned, and have a right to be released from them.

14. Imperfect piety or love on the part of the dying person necessarily brings with it great fear; and the smaller the love, the greater the fear.

15. This fear or horror is sufficient in itself, to say nothing of other things, to constitute the penalty of purgatory, since it is very near to the horror of despair.

16. Hell, purgatory, and heaven seem to differ the same as despair, fear, and assurance of salvation.

17. It seems as though for the souls in purgatory fear should necessarily decrease and love increase.

18. Furthermore, it does not seem proved, either by reason or by Scripture, that souls in purgatory are outside the state of merit, that is, unable to grow in love.

19. Nor does it seem proved that souls in purgatory, at least not all

of them, are certain and assured of their own salvation, even if we ourselves may be entirely certain of it.

20. Therefore the pope, when he uses the words "plenary remission of all penalties," does not actually mean "all penalties," but only those imposed by himself.

21. Thus those indulgence preachers are in error who say that a man is absolved from every penalty and saved by papal indulgences.

22. As a matter of fact, the pope remits to souls in purgatory no penalty which, according to canon law, they should have paid in this life.

23. If remission of all penalties whatsoever could be granted to anyone at all, certainly it would be granted only to the most perfect, that is, to very few.

24. For this reason most people are necessarily deceived by that indiscriminate and high-sounding promise of release from penalty.

25. That power which the pope has in general over purgatory corresponds to the power which any bishop or curate has in a particular way in his own diocese and parish.

26. The pope does very well when he grants remission to souls in purgatory, not by the power of the keys, which he does not have, but by way of intercession for them.

27. They preach only human doctrines who say that as soon as the money clinks into the money chest, the soul flies out of purgatory.

28. It is certain that when money clinks in the money chest, greed and avarice can be increased; but when the church intercedes, the result is in the hands of God alone.

29. Who knows whether all souls in purgatory wish to be redeemed, since we have exceptions in St. Severinus and St. Paschal, as related in a legend – which tells of two saints who

were willing to remain in torment to suffer for others.

30. No one is sure of the integrity of his own contrition, much less of having received plenary remission.

31. The man who actually buys indulgences is as rare as he who is really penitent; indeed, he is exceedingly rare.

32. Those who believe that they can be certain of their salvation because they have indulgence letters will be eternally damned, together with their teachers.

33. Men must especially be on guard against those who say that the pope's pardons are that inestimable gift of God by which man is reconciled to him.

34. For the graces of indulgences are concerned only with the penalties of sacramental satisfaction established by man.

35. They who teach that contrition is not necessary on the part of those who intend to buy souls out of purgatory or to buy confessional privileges preach unchristian doctrine.

36. Any truly repentant Christian has a right to full remission of penalty and guilt, even without indulgence letters.

37. Any true Christian, whether living or dead, participates in all the blessings of Christ and the church; and this is granted him by God, even without indulgence letters.

38. Nevertheless, papal remission and blessing are by no means to be disregarded, for they are, as I have said (Thesis 6), the proclamation of the divine remission.

39. It is very difficult, even for the most learned theologians, at one and the same time to commend to the people the bounty of indulgences and the need of true contrition.

40. A Christian who is truly contrite seeks and loves to pay penalties for his sins; the bounty of indulgences, however, relaxes penalties and causes men to hate them - at least it furnishes occasion for hating them.

41. Papal indulgences must be preached with caution, lest people

erroneously think that they are preferable to other good works of love.

42. Christians are to be taught that the pope does not intend that the buying of indulgences should in any way be compared with works of mercy.

43. Christians are to be taught that he who gives to the poor or lends to the needy does a better deed than he who buys indulgences.

44. Because love grows by works of love, man thereby becomes better. Man does not, however, become better by means of indulgences but is merely freed from penalties.

45. Christians are to be taught that he who sees a needy man and passes him by, yet gives his money for indulgences, does not buy papal indulgences but God's wrath.

46. Christians are to be taught that, unless they have more than they need, they must reserve enough for their family needs and by no means squander it on indulgences.

47. Christians are to be taught that they buying of indulgences is a matter of free choice, not commanded.

48. Christians are to be taught that the pope, in granting indulgences, needs and thus desires their devout prayer more than their money.

49. Christians are to be taught that papal indulgences are useful only if they do not put their trust in them, but very harmful if they lose their fear of God because of them.

50. Christians are to be taught that if the pope knew the exactions of the indulgence preachers, he would rather that the basilica of St. Peter were burned to ashes than built up with the skin, flesh, and bones of his sheep.

51. Christians are to be taught that the pope would and should wish to give of his own money, even though he had to sell the basilica of St. Peter, to many of those from whom certain

hawkers of indulgences cajole money.

52. It is vain to trust in salvation by indulgence letters, even though the indulgence commissary, or even the pope, were to offer his soul as security.

53. They are the enemies of Christ and the pope who forbid altogether the preaching of the Word of God in some churches in order that indulgences may be preached in others.

54. Injury is done to the Word of God when, in the same sermon, an equal or larger amount of time is devoted to indulgences than to the Word.

55. It is certainly the pope's sentiment that if indulgences, which are a very insignificant thing, are celebrated with one bell, one procession, and one ceremony, then the gospel, which is the very greatest thing, should be preached with a hundred bells, a hundred processions, a hundred ceremonies.

56. The true treasures of the church, out of which the pope distributes indulgences, are not sufficiently discussed or known among the people of Christ.

57. That indulgences are not temporal treasures is certainly clear, for many indulgence sellers do not distribute them freely but only gather them.

58. Nor are they the merits of Christ and the saints, for, even without the pope, the latter always work grace for the inner man, and the cross, death, and hell for the outer man.

59. St. Lawrence said that the poor of the church were the treasures of the church, but he spoke according to the usage of the word in his own time.

60. Without want of consideration we say that the keys of the church, given by the merits of Christ, are that treasure.

61. For it is clear that the pope's power is of itself sufficient for the remission of penalties and cases reserved by himself.

62. The true treasure of the church is the most holy gospel of the

glory and grace of God.

63. But this treasure is naturally most odious, for it makes the first to be last (Matt.20:16).

64. On the other hand, the treasure of indulgences is naturally most acceptable, for it makes the last to be first.

65. Therefore the treasures of the gospel are nets with which one formerly fished for men of wealth.

66. The treasures of indulgences are nets with which one now fishes for the wealth of men.

67. The indulgences which the demagogues acclaim as the greatest graces are actually understood to be such only insofar as they promote gain.

68. They are nevertheless in truth the most insignificant graces when compared with the grace of God and the piety of the cross.

69. Bishops and curates are bound to admit the commissaries of papal indulgences with all reverence.

70. But they are much more bound to strain their eyes and ears lest these men preach their own dreams instead of what the pope has commissioned.

71. Let him who speaks against the truth concerning papal indulgences be anathema and accursed.

72. But let him who guards against the lust and license of the indulgence preachers be blessed.

73. Just as the pope justly thunders against those who by any means whatever contrive harm to the sale of indulgences.

74. Much more does he intend to thunder against those who use indulgences as a pretext to contrive harm to holy love and truth.

75. To consider papal indulgences so great that they could absolve a man even if he had done the impossible and had violated the mother of God is madness.

76. We say on the contrary that papal indulgences cannot remove the very least of venial sins as far as guilt is concerned.

77. To say that even St. Peter if he were now pope, could not grant greater graces is blasphemy against St. Peter and the pope.

78. We say on the contrary that even the present pope, or any pope whatsoever, has greater graces at his disposal, that is, the gospel, spiritual powers, gifts of healing, etc., as it is written. (1 Cor.12:28)

79. To say that the cross emblazoned with the papal coat of arms, and set up by the indulgence preachers is equal in worth to the cross of Christ is blasphemy.

80. The bishops, curates, and theologians who permit such talk to be spread among the people will have to answer for this.

81. This unbridled preaching of indulgences makes it difficult even for learned men to rescue the reverence which is due the pope from slander or from the shrewd questions of the laity.

82. Such as: "Why does not the pope empty purgatory for the sake of holy love and the dire need of the souls that are there if he redeems an infinite number of souls for the sake of miserable money with which to build a church?" The former reason would be most just; the latter is most trivial.

83. Again, "Why are funeral and anniversary masses for the dead continued and why does he not return or permit the withdrawal of the endowments founded for them, since it is wrong to pray for the redeemed?"

84. Again, "What is this new piety of God and the pope that for a consideration of money they permit a man who is impious and their enemy to buy out of purgatory the pious soul of a friend of God and do not rather, because of the need of that pious and beloved soul, free it for pure love's sake?"

85. Again, "Why are the penitential canons, long since abrogated and dead in actual fact and through disuse, now satisfied by

the granting of indulgences as though they were still alive and in force?"

86. Again, "Why does not the pope, whose wealth is today greater than the wealth of the richest Crassus, build this one basilica of St. Peter with his own money rather than with the money of poor believers?"

87. Again, "What does the pope remit or grant to those who by perfect contrition already have a right to full remission and blessings?"

88. Again, "What greater blessing could come to the church than if the pope were to bestow these remissions and blessings on every believer a hundred times a day, as he now does but once?"

89. Since the pope seeks the salvation of souls rather than money by his indulgences, why does he suspend the indulgences and pardons previously granted when they have equal efficacy?

90. To repress these very sharp arguments of the laity by force alone, and not to resolve them by giving reasons, is to expose the church and the pope to the ridicule of their enemies and to make Christians unhappy.

91. If, therefore, indulgences were preached according to the spirit and intention of the pope, all these doubts would be readily resolved. Indeed, they would not exist.

92. Away, then, with all those prophets who say to the people of Christ, "Peace, peace," and there is no peace! (Jer.6:14)

93. Blessed be all those prophets who say to the people of Christ, "Cross, cross," and there is no cross!

94. Christians should be exhorted to be diligent in following Christ, their Head, through penalties, death and hell.

95. And thus be confident of entering into heaven through many tribulations rather than through the false security of peace (Acts 14:22).

Appendix 2: Luther's Speech at the Imperial Diet in Worms, Germany (April 1521)

In April 1521, Luther appeared before Emperor Charles V to defend what he had taught and written.

Most Serene Emperor, Illustrious Princes, Gracious Lords:

I this day appear before you in all humility, according to your command, and I implore your majesty and your august highnesses, by the mercies of God, to listen with favour to the defence of a cause which I am well assured is just and right. I ask pardon, if by reason of my ignorance, I am wanting in the manners that befit a court; for I have not been brought up in king's palaces, but in the seclusion of a cloister; and I claim no other merit than that of having spoken and written with the simplicity of mind which regards nothing but the glory of God and the pure instruction of the people of Christ.

Two questions were yesterday put to me by his imperial majesty; the first, whether I was the author of the books whose titles were read; the second, whether I wished to revoke or defend the doctrine I have taught. I answered the first directly, and I adhere to that answer: that these books are mine and published by me, except so far as they may have been altered or interpolated by the craft or officiousness of opponents. As for the second question, I am now about to reply to it; and I must first entreat your Majesty and your Highnesses to deign to consider that I have composed writings on very different subjects. In some I have discussed Faith and Good Works, in a spirit at once so pure, clear, and Christian, that even my adversaries themselves, far from finding anything to censure, confess that these writings are profitable, and deserve to be perused by devout persons. The pope's bull, violent as

71

it is, acknowledges this. What, then, should I be doing if I were now to retract these writings? Wretched man! I alone, of all men living, should be abandoning truths approved by the unanimous voice of friends and enemies, and should be opposing doctrines that the whole world glories in confessing!

I have composed, secondly, certain works against the papacy, wherein I have attacked such as by false doctrines, irregular lives, and scandalous examples, afflict the Christian world, and ruin the bodies and souls of men. And is not this confirmed by the grief of all who fear God? Is it not manifest that the laws and human doctrines of the popes entangle, vex, and distress the consciences of the faithful, while the crying and endless extortions of Rome engulf the property and wealth of Christendom, and more particularly of this illustrious nation? Yet it is a perpetual statute that the laws and doctrines of the pope be held erroneous and reprobate when they are contrary to the Gospel and the opinions of the church fathers.

If I were to revoke what I have written on that subject, what should I do but strengthen this tyranny, and open a wider door to so many and flagrant impieties? Bearing down all resistance with fresh fury, we should behold these proud men swell, foam, and rage more than ever! And not merely would the yoke which now weighs down Christians be made more grinding by my retraction it would thereby become, so to speak, lawful, for, by my retraction, it would receive confirmation from your most serene majesty, and all the States of the Empire. Great God! I should thus be like to an infamous cloak, used to hide and cover over every kind of malice and tyranny.

In the third and last place, I have written some books against private individuals, who had undertaken to defend the tyranny of Rome by destroying the faith. I freely confess that I may have attacked such persons with more violence than was consistent with my profession as an ecclesiastic: I do not think of myself as a saint; but neither can I retract these books. Because I should, by so doing, sanction the impieties of my opponents, and they would thence take occasion to crush God's people with still more cruelty.

Yet, as I am a mere man, and not God, I will defend myself after the example of Jesus Christ, who said: "If I have spoken evil, bear witness against me; but if well, why dost thou strike me?"?(John xviii:23). How much more should I, who am but dust and ashes, and so prone to error, desire that every one should bring forward what he can against my doctrine. Therefore, most serene emperor, and you illustrious princes, and all, whether high or low, who hear me, I implore you by the mercies of God to prove to me by the writings of the prophets and apostles that I am in error. As soon as I shall be convinced, I will instantly retract all my errors, and will myself be the first to seize my writings, and commit them to the flames.

What I have just said will, I think, clearly show that I have well considered and weighed, not only the dangers to which I am exposing myself, but also the parties and dissensions excited in the world by means of my doctrine, of which I was yesterday so gravely admonished. But far from being dismayed by them, I rejoice exceedingly to see the Gospel this day, as of old, a cause of disturbance and disagreement; for such is the character and destiny of God's word. "I came not to send peace unto the earth, but a sword," said Jesus Christ. "For I am come to set a man at variance against his father, and the daughter against her mother, and the daughter-in-law against her mother-in-law; and a man's foes shall be those of his own household." (Matthew x:34-36)

God is wonderful and terrible in His counsels. Let us have a care, lest in our endeavours to arrest discords, we be bound to fight against the holy word of God and bring down upon our heads a frightful deluge of inextricable dangers, present disaster, and everlasting desolations. Let us have a care that the reign of the young and noble prince, the Emperor Charles, on whom, next to God, we build so many hopes, should not only commence, but continue and terminate its course, under the most favourable auspices.

I might cite examples drawn from the oracles of God. I might speak of Pharaohs, of kings of Babylon, or of Israel, who were never more contributing to their own ruin than when, by measures in appearances most prudent, they thought to establish their authority! God removeth the mountains and they know not (Job ix:5). In speaking thus, I do not suppose that such noble princes have need of my poor judgment; but I wish to acquit myself of a duty whose fulfilment my native Germany has a right to expect from her children. And so commending myself to your august majesty, and your most serene highnesses, I beseech you in all humility, not to permit the hatred of my enemies to rain upon me an indignation I have not deserved. I have done.

[*Having delivered this speech in German, Luther was now asked to repeat it in Latin. After some hesitation, he did so. He was then reminded that he should answer a simple question: whether he would retract or not. Thus he continued:*]

Since your most serene majesty and your high mightinesses require of me a simple, clear and direct answer, I will give one, and it is this: I cannot submit my faith either to the pope or to the council, because it is as clear as noonday that they have fallen into error and even into glaring inconsistency with themselves. If, then, I am not convinced by proof from Holy Scripture, or by cogent reasons, if I am not satisfied by the very text I have cited, and if my judgment is not in this way brought into subjection to God's word, I neither can nor will retract anything; for it cannot be either safe or honest for a Christian to speak against his conscience. Here I stand; I cannot do otherwise; God help me! Amen.

"Unless I am convinced by the testimony of the Holy Scriptures or by evident reason-for I can believe neither pope nor councils alone, as it is clear that they have erred repeatedly and contradicted themselves-I consider myself convicted by the testimony of Holy Scripture, which is my basis; my conscience is captive to the Word of God. Thus I cannot and will not recant, because acting against one's conscience is neither safe nor sound. [Here I stand; I can do no other.]* God help me. Amen."

Also by Andy McIlree

Garments for Glory
The Five Solas of the Reformation

About the Author

Andy was born in Glasgow, Scotland, He came to know the Lord in 1954, and was baptized in 1958. He is married to Anna, and he lives in Kilmacolm, Scotland. They have two daughters and one son. He entered into full-time service in 1976 with the churches of God (www.churchesofgod.info). He has engaged in an itinerant ministry in western countries and has been privileged to serve the Lord in India and Myanmar (formerly Burma).

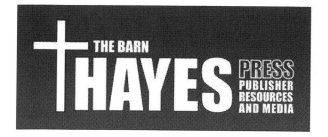

About the Publisher

Hayes Press (www.hayespress.org) is a registered charity in the United Kingdom, whose primary mission is to disseminate the Word of God, mainly through literature. It is one of the largest distributors of gospel tracts and leaflets in the United Kingdom, with over 100 titles and hundreds of thousands despatched annually. In addition to paperbacks and eBooks, Hayes Press also publishes Plus Eagles Wings, a fun and educational Bible magazine for children, and Golden Bells, a popular daily Bible reading calendar in wall or desk formats. Also available are over 100 Bibles in many different versions, shapes and sizes, Bible text posters and much more!